As a pastor's daughter who's struggled her whole life with institutionalized religion, *Bandersnatch* breathes new life into these dry bones. Erika Morrison has unveiled the heart of Ezekial 37; her words are the
breath of God on the body of the church, a manual of freedom for the
religiously oppressed. *Bandersnatch* is the transfiguration of Christ for
an unbelieving generation and a prophetic word for those thirsty for
revival. It is an honor to endorse this very important work.

—EMILY T. WIERENGA, FOUNDER OF THE LULU TREE AND AUTHOR OF
ATLAS GIRL AND *MAKING IT HOME* (WWW.EMILYWIERENGA.COM)

To know Erika Morrison is to love the way she dares you to be more
fully yourself. A woman who listens closely to the heartbeat of God for
his people, she is unafraid to embrace the beautiful uniqueness found in
each one of us. Erika oozes individuality and deep-seeded wisdom in a
way that inspires us to listen and dig further within our own souls. She
is a true friend who desires nothing more than to see the body of
Christ walk into fullness as we each embrace exactly who God created
us to be.

—LOGAN WOLFRAM, AUTHOR OF *CURIOUS FAITH*,
SPEAKER, CEO OF ALLUME MINISTRIES

Seeing Christianity through Erika Morrison's eyes is like cliff-diving
into a lagoon after a lifetime of municipal pools. Her stories and in-
sights on a creative kingdom life are unlike anything I've encountered
in my evangelical background, and they can't help but tug out a re-
sponsive joy from the deepest parts of our identities. *Bandersnatch* is the
antidote to "normal" we never knew we needed.

—BETHANY BASSETT, WRITER AND EDITOR

A decade plus of surrender to God's unearthing of her own peculiar,
internal architecture has given Erika profound insight to whisper into
other hearts and spiritual journeys. Erika's prose reads like the most
poignant poems and songs, and has become a powerful tool in the hand
of the Father as he continues to excavate my own truest heart.

—DANA BUTLER, MAMA OF LITTLES, WORSHIP
PASTOR, AND WRITER AT DANALBUTLER.COM

Erika's account of spiritual development flows as an underground stream that feeds the pump, not as neatly packaged bottles of water.

—MARY CADNEY, OKLAHOMA ARTIST

Bandersnatch is a hole torn open in the fabric of ordinary earth, offering a dazzling glimpse of the kingdom breaking through. In its pages, Erika Morrison relentlessly intertwines electric currents of poetry, faith, and the raw honesty of her unconventionally beautiful heart. Not many books have captured the otherworldly but so very real essence of the magical, mystical reality of walking with the Spirit in the footsteps of Jesus like this one has. *Bandersnatch* makes me want to dance, dream, create, commune, pray, die, and live again from the very core of my chest.

—MICAH MURRAY, WRITER AT MICAHJMURRAY.COM

Erika is not simply a writer—she is an artist. In *Bandersnatch,* she creates this glorious space where I am reintroduced to myself, my true self. Then she gives me a virtual hug and the permission to go be that self. This is, I think, what the most wonderful books always do. They remind us who we truly are.

—SHAWN SMUCKER, AUTHOR OF *BUILDING A LIFE OUT OF WORDS*

Erika Morrison is one to watch if you want to know what it looks like to live infused with a sense of adventure and surrender. She is a teacher in the practice of engaging God with all your quirk and senses. I love the way she exemplifies a worshiper of Christ, how she keeps her eyes peeled for glory in plain sight. If there ever were a Bandersnatch, it would be her, and I want to live "crossed-over" how she does. Better yet, I want to live avant-garde like Christ.

—AMBER C. HAINES, AUTHOR OF *WILD IN THE HOLLOW*

With the fervor of a prophet, the creativity of a performance artist, the fierce lioness of a mother, and the dusty feet of a disciple, Erika is the embodiment of life outside the narrow boundary markers. She is a breath of fresh air in a stale room, a voice I trust, a tender heart, and a bracing wind. Open the door to her Spirit-led influence and you will never be the same.

—SARAH BESSEY, AUTHOR OF *JESUS FEMINIST* AND *OUT OF SORTS*

AN INVITATION TO EXPLORE YOUR
UNCONVENTIONAL SOUL

ERIKA MORRISON

W PUBLISHING GROUP

AN IMPRINT OF THOMAS NELSON

Published in Nashville, Tennessee, by Thomas Nelson. Thomas Nelson is a registered trademark of HarperCollins Christian Publishing, Inc.

Published in association with the literary agency D. C. Jacobson & Associates, LLC, an Author Management Company, www.dcjacobson.com.

Thomas Nelson, Inc., titles may be purchased in bulk for educational, business, fund-raising, or sales promotional use. For information, please email SpecialMarkets@ThomasNelson.com.

Library of Congress Control Number: 2015908305

ISBN 978-0-7180-3622-5

Printed in the United States of America

15 16 17 18 19 20 RRD 6 5 4 3 2 1

For Austin

"She runs so fearfully quick. You might as well try to catch a Bandersnatch!"

—LEWIS CARROLL, *THROUGH THE LOOKING-GLASS*

Contents

Contents

Art

FOREWORD

As I read *Bandersnatch*, I found myself feeling all too much at home in the Christian establishment or institution to which Erika often refers in this book. I admit that, at my worst, I am capable of fostering a cultural monopoly of the Faith—unconsciously bringing to bear on unsuspecting followers the bonds that come with that controlling worldview. *Bandersnatch* reminds me that I must be constantly vigilant in that regard.

Nevertheless, as someone who feels called to be a steward of the establishment, I find myself indebted to a long train of truth-seekers who have had thoughts as profound as those found in these pages. I believe that, at its best, the institution of Christianity seeks to collate the myriad stories and theories into an unbroken commentary, hoping to present a seamless continuity of thought and ritual that is worthy of a two-thousand-year-old tradition. However, rather than seamlessness, the "seams" more often than not become visible. Those seams are a part of the history of Christianity, and while potentially either transformative or destructive, they tend not to be easy times in the life of the Faith. *Bandersnatch* is right in suggesting that we in the West are living on top of one such seam, and that the transition may be trickier to navigate than most of us think. More importantly, it reminds us that there are spiritual refugees who are caught in the liminal place between the old which is not working, and the new which has not yet been fully realized. This is a difficult place for spirituality to survive, much less thrive. It is in times like these that unconventional thinkers like Erika are invaluable to the rest of us—both to those caught on that seam and those of us who may confuse tradition with conformity. For such a time as this, we need the voice of the unconventional.

I find that unconventional thinkers come in two varieties. The first I call the *archetypes*, and they are seminal characters who few of us ever have a chance to cross paths with. They are often profound theorists and activists who inspire us, albeit from a distance. Their voices are like those of the biblical figure John the Baptist, who stood on the margins and called for change, but due to their distance, they can seldom model for us the day-to-day lifestyle that their nonconformity advocates. While I am thankful for those types, and the spasm of inspiration they provide, I need a closer guide.

This is where the second type of avant-garde thinker comes in. They declare the new direction while also showing us the fresh rhythms and rituals that may line the way. They seem to carry a burden that drives them to not only personally experience the wrestling that brings one through the liminal place, but feel constrained to turn to those of us still caught in the fray and offer their findings. They are the breath of wind needed for so many of us who are crossing through the spiritual doldrums found in the liminal passage. They are the voice of the Spirit within culture for those of us called to steward the establishment. We should seek them out, and listen closely to their words.

Bandersnatch came out of who Erika is, and her need to steward the seam between what is not working for so many, and the new expression where they can find a home. I am thankful for the unconventional prophets like Erika who, upon finding the new, know that their experience must remain linked to community, and they circle back to the rest of us.

May it build your confidence in reading these pages to know that an unconventional spirit like Erika invited an establishment steward to write the foreword. That act alone demonstrates the tremendous security and freedom that she has attained during the crossover she discusses in these pages. I commend her thoughts and experiences to you, in all of their unconventionality, as a prophet's voice that so many of us need to hear.

James Ehrman
—Executive Director, Love146
Associate Research Fellow,
Rivendell Institute at Yale University

WHY *BANDERSNATCH*?

Bandersnatch was first introduced to the English language by Lewis Carroll, when he penned his children's classic *Through the Looking-Glass* and later in various other works.

A bandersnatch, while more commonly known as the wild, ferocious, mythical creature of Carroll's creation, has also been defined in modern terms as a person with uncouth or unconventional habits and attitudes, even as someone considered to be a bit of a troublemaker or nuisance. Mix all these definitions together and on the surface it looks like we have a mostly bad personality on our hands.

Does this make you wonder why I would want to take an almost-always-negative noun and use it as the title and theme for my book? Let me explain: In the 2010 Disney film adaptation of *Alice in Wonderland*, the bandersnatch, along with most of the other underworld creatures, was trapped in captivity to the evil Red Queen. Their true natures were suppressed from the dark cloud of her tyrannical rule and from the constant threat of getting beheaded if they didn't toe her rules and regime to the exact letter. But when Alice falls down the rabbit hole and discovers that her purpose for being in Wonderland is to fulfill the prophecy of overthrowing the oppressive systems of the Red

Queen, she commits several impossible acts of bravery to achieve that objective. When that objective is met, the power of the Red Queen's evil empire dissolves, the bondage over all the creatures is broken, and they return to their bona fide identities, including the bandersnatch.

While the bandersnatch is still a rather untamed and frightening beast with unpredictable habits and unconventional attitudes, *he is also good* because his fierceness, his troublemaking, his nuisance-bearing disposition is now submitted to a better cause—the dominion of the kind and good White Queen.

Keeping that story in mind, this book is an invitation to turn the word into a verb. I'm inviting you to bandersnatch, that is, to acknowledge and embrace the unconventional habits and attitudes that are your birthright, to grapple with what has dominion over you, and to become a bit of a nuisance to the unhelpful, unhealthy, and often harmful systems of the human-made kingdom. Within the process I believe you will begin to reimagine your very own soul and its unique outpourings in the world, to jump into your singular skin, to discover and live as your "true self."

Your true self, in its purest form, is what I would define as a love affair between God and your only, inherent DNA. When the Spirit of God and the soul of you have a meeting within your body, what gets born again and again and again is your true self, your true identity. The false self is the part of you that is born from your ego and functions separately from divine accord.

I believe one of the central endeavors of the human experience is to consciously discover the intimacies of who we already are. As in: life is not about building an alternate name for ourselves; it's about discovering the name we already have.

But how do we begin (or continue) the process of unearthing the truth of our intrinsic selves? Most people I know have intentionally invested in some form of self-discovery for some period of time. And yet, how many of us feel we could put language around the parameters of our uncommon inner workings? If I asked you to, could you raise your hand right now and say unequivocally, "This is who I am" or "I am this"?

I'm not talking about your ability to tell me what your job is or your confidence in saying "I am a child of God." What I am asking is this: Within the framework of being a child of God, what part of God do you represent? Do you know where you begin and where you end? Do you know the here-to-here of your uniqueness? Do you know, as John Duns Scotus puts it, your unusual, individual "thisness"?[1]

Before we move on and in the quietness of your own heart, I think it's important to ask yourself, *Do I know the words that describe who I am?*

It shouldn't be that hard, but it often is. And though we can never lose our true selves, those selves can get buried under all kinds of horsefeathers and hogwash, stuff and senselessness, and we can fall short of grasping, comprehending, or realizing who we really are.

And why is that, do you suppose? If we each have a unique blueprint coded and stitched right into our singular cells, why can't we seem to put a finger to it and catch our own pulse? What do you imagine our identities are buried beneath?

I don't think it's a stretch to say that the great boring and blaring voices of mainstream culture have made whole oppressive systems out of what it means to be a human, what it means to be normal, how exactly everyone should follow the status quo—A plus B plus believe this and "buy me" makes you perfect and pretty and successful. Since the beginning of time, societies have created their own organized schemes, methods, and rules, erecting power structures and telling individuals to live by them.

Layer upon layer upon layer of systems and rules and how-tos have piled up over thousands and thousands of years until human institutions are so thick and heavy and spinning so fast, we don't even know that what we've been born into is not the truth—at least not the whole truth, or the better truth.

We don't know that as soon as we make our appearance on this perilous and precious planet, we are downloaded with a virus-like infrastructure that begins the takeover process. From that moment we are flooded with voices that scream "Do this don't do that don't be you don't be you don't be you!" Our constitutional design is the most natural part of us, but it's also the part of us that can't hear itself think (much less breathe or bloom) amidst the din of culture conformity. And before long, it all feels . . . normal.

Without even knowing what's happening, we end up subscribed to systems that are fundamentally at odds with our purpose of harmonizing with God. We live our lives bent under a low, artificial, and suffocating ceiling, having given away parts—or the near entirety—of our selves to the systems and institutions that persistently pound into our skulls what they deem is the truth of us.

Look out your window, open your door, drive down the billboarded highway at eighty miles an hour, walk into the giant spread of a shopping mall, turn on your TV, and see what values and systems are being promoted, which aspects of humanity are celebrated. Realize what you've bought into, what contracts you've signed with your own lifeblood.

This is bondage to the debts of humanity. And now, just as ever before, I look around me and I see that we tend to live according to the will of mere mortals instead of the will we were born for; then we go about our dogged and dog-eat-dog days wondering why we can't keep a flame lit inside us or don't have the birthright of our own peculiar—as in particular—wholeness to work with.

If we all take an intimate look at the percentages, maybe we'll realize how much we are owned.

We are owned.

And <u>human-made systems are taking up space where our identity should be blooming</u>.

Human-made systems take up space where identity should be blooming.

But identity is a living organism, and it wants to grow.

And just so we're clear about what a system is: a human-made system is a boxed-tight set of beliefs, rules, formulas, and assumptions. It's a social structure or scheme created by humanity—as opposed to created by God—that governs our behavior.

Let me say that again: a human-made system is a boxed set of beliefs, rules, formulas, a social structure or scheme that governs our behavior.

Is a human-made system always and intrinsically evil? No. And it's probably inevitable anyway because we humans, it seems, can't keep from trying to get organized. Systemized. The problem comes when we organize and systemize to the point and at the expense of being able to function within our own God-made dynamic and original design—and especially when we let our true, God-invented selves be co-opted by these human inventions, forgetting who we were created to be.

In the context of complex social systems, the term *institution* is also used to describe this power structure that hijacks our consciousness. And getting bogged down and boxed in with human-made systems is what we would call "becoming institutionalized." Which looks a lot like robotic, herd-mentality habits, actions, and attitudes rather than unconventional, uncommon, and unique habits, actions, and attitudes.

The systems, full of vacuity and necessary conformity, are inappropriate and abusive substitutes for oneness with God.

And we might wonder why we have zero energy left with which to nurture a full-hearted awareness of our God-gifted uniqueness? We've contracted too much of it away for the absolutes of nothing. We've complied and consented, and the cost has been high. The energy we've intentionally or inadvertently dumped into the systems isn't available anymore to help develop and discern our true selves.

Bandersnatch is an invitation to begin dismantling what imprisons you by beginning to identify the false noises in your ears, defying the tyrannical power structures that own pieces of you, and breaking the boundaries that contain and inform your biological and spiritual DNA.

Bandersnatch is also about learning not to be a chameleon. It's about positive nonconformity, about not robbing the body of Christ of your DNA. Because Jesus was born into the whirlpool, too, but every single audacious and seemingly ridiculous thing he did was to reverse the direction of the current, reshape the landscape, bring a kingdom of heaven economy into the wasteland of our wearying machinations. As if to say: be thoughtful, careful, intentional with your one dear life because it appears you don't get another.

The Holy Spirit is a surprise, the ultimate nonconformist—subverter of the normal way of seeing and doing and being. How scandalous! And whenever and wherever possible, we would do well not to house-train the Spirit. Not even try, for the Spirit-Wind blows where it will, and "you have no idea where it comes from or where it's headed next" (John 3:8).

Imagine for me what it would mean to all the other intersections of your life—faith, family, personal and communal mission, and so on—if your clean, blooming, and rarified identity, your identity minus the trespassing human-made not-qualities, were to overflow and fall down from the essence of you.

So who are you, stripped of those things that tell you who you are?

Have you been conditioned by the voices of a society that tell us to be a certain this way or that way, their way or not at all?

Or do you and your values come from your own original cells and nerves, initiative and ingenuity?

Bandersnatch is about finding the elements, features, and aspects of ourselves that allow us to design life with peculiar flair. It is about being permissioned and invited to reimagine the approach to exploring and realizing personal identity, about embracing a deep-seated belief in our own rarity, about knowing our part in the great interlocking circle of contribution, an interlocking circle that mirrors the final face of glory—as opposed to the oppressive systems of humanity.

Are you with me?

Having said that, I couldn't very easily follow my own values if I were to write you a formulaic how-to book. I have an automatic aversion to such things because I see that we've done a brilliant job in our culture of systemizing transformation and growth.

My natural tendency is to be subversive and nondirective in my writing, but my editorial team tells me that this can create a cumbersome reading experience. So I will teach and lead in this *Bandersnatch* work, and you will hear me be directive at different points throughout. But never will I tout myself as an expert who sits in a lofty position, giving you the exact ingredients for baking your life to perfection.

Instead, I offer you the results of my own bandersnatch adventures. I dove deep inside myself to write it and excavated the truest parts and things and narratives I know. I offer them to

Today I was asked to name what makes me unique, drives me, different? I couldn't answer
10/17/15

you in a spirit of flow and fluidity—whirling, amoebic movement that I hope will inspire an original, organic, metamorphic process in you, a journey unique to you and your individual history, organisms, and experiences.

One more thing. My own nature, I've learned, has been calibrated with a high capacity for intimacy. So I hope as you're reading this book that you'll imagine we're sitting fireside and we've got mugs of something. I might even be in my bathrobe and slippers, without makeup, my hair undone. So our time together will be profoundly personal, a little messy perhaps, and also, I hope, transformative.

Will you hold my hand and join me? Just reach through your time and the space between us and take my fingers, and I'll take yours.

I love walking with people. I love the adventure and the process.

And: you.

>>

1

NEW WOR[L]D ORDER

When the Virgin Mary pushed the crown of God's head into the hay, when Jesus came as a babe onto this orbiting globe, a new kingdom order was birthed along with his slippery skin, and his first squalling cry rewrote the human lexicon. The earth turned over, and all the systems and traditions of humankind went cattywampus with the entrance of the infant whose tiny shoulders suddenly carried the government of the world. Since that day two thousand and some odd years ago, the sincere worshipers who trail behind his dusty feet have been on the hunt to understand all the ways this one Christ-man changed the game.

And change the game he did, with all his talk of losing to gain, the meek inheriting the earth, and the last getting exalted as first. It seems that on the other side of Jesus, so many things and thoughts are the exact opposite of definitions already established in that day and age. Or at the very least, the definitions he imprinted are designed and emphasized to have more fullness, a different shape, or a new objective.

Taking a cue from my friend Johnny, I have begun referring to this redefining, fulfilling process as "crossing over." Crossing over is the antidote to the systems and traditions of humankind and simply means that a word or an idea or a value has made the journey from being defined by and rooted in the world to being defined by and rooted in Jesus—his ancient birth, life, and death on a cross. You might've noticed that I've already taken the liberty of "crossing over" the word *bandersnatch*.

One of the earliest words I can perceive Jesus crossing over was *king*. Many of his Jewish contemporaries were looking for a deliverer who would lead an army, a strong-armed king with a long-sweeping sword to rescue their race from centuries of oppression. But Jesus turned *king* upside-down when he poured his infinite body into infant's skin and landed in a peasant's feed trough next to the dung heaps of lowing cattle. His only scepter was a fistful of straw; his royal garment was a square of textile with a diaper-like shape. And as an adult, he was the king who went low, bent at the knees over a bowl of water with the feet of his followers between his fingers. He set aside the privileges of kingship and assumed the status of a slave. And with that redefining act, he imprinted the fabric of the universe with a previously unheard definition for royalty.

Jesus is the curtain that blows in the breeze between this world and the next, and getting ourselves as close as possible to his torn body will help us see and hear and taste and feel and know the living, spinning terms that give every little microscopic thing its brimming, abundant definition.

In other words, the Curtain is ripped, y'all. Heaven is just behind the cosmic tear. Christ's flesh is the gateway to understanding how the kingdom defines what it means to be a human living on this earth while bringing divine circumstances into the here and now. On this side of those folds of Jesus-cloth are the earth terms, and on the other side are the heaven terms, and here we are with our feet planted in the dirt but our arms stretching up through the cosmos.

The tension of all the terms—held in the human and divine paradox of Jesus Christ—is now being met in our bodies as we labor to pull the worlds together for a meeting of skin and celestial. A collision of realities, so to speak.

But Jesus is not in competition with the earth's terms; it's not necessary for the earth's terms to be wrong in order for Jesus' to be right or vice versa. This isn't an either-or ideological war, but rather a space to breathe in the free air of paradoxical both-and. What the earth offers just isn't the whole story. The earth only has one-half of the paradox and Jesus has the other, and although they often seem to contradict, I believe they are designed to live in tension to one another. Each gives its counterpart the integrity and brimming value of its full definition, its full truth.

So we keep asking and seeking and knocking and reaching because we are hungry to know the burgeoning scope of everything. Do you feel it too—the ache in your belly to know that truth? Do you find yourself continually asking and seeking and knocking and reaching because you are hungry to feast on bigger and better and crossed-over paradigms?

Maybe this thought has come into your thinking space before. Have you already walked through a life story or situation where what you'd always thought or been told didn't inform or encompass the totality of your reality anymore and you found your understanding for that thing "cross over" to the other side of Jesus?

It would've felt something like an aha moment, filled with wildness and wonder. In real time you would have seen your glasses being defogged and wiped clean and with the bright new view you might have sensed your molecules shifting to places they were born to be.

For me, this crossing-over process all started with the word *bless*, a word we are very familiar with in our society and faith culture, a word that generally conjures up feelings of goodness, happiness, and contentment, maybe even wealth, health, or success. Our society informs us that being blessed looks like a two-car garage, a white picket fence, two-point-five good-looking, healthy kids, and perhaps a dog or two. Our faith culture has entire congregations wrapped around the finger of prosperity under the guise of "God's blessing." And while both examples of *bless* may be accurate applications of the word, they certainly don't represent the entirety of the narrative.

When I was twenty-four, my Christian worldview was short on experience and shy on wisdom. I thought all those aforementioned surface things were exactly what it meant to be blessed. But while I had the "perfect" husband and three gorgeous kids in good condition, I wasn't entirely satisfied with our level of "blessing," especially when it came to finances. Our circumstances didn't allow for us to do things we dreamed to do or be the people we wanted to be. And it wasn't as if we were yearning for designer clothes and fancy cars. Many of our dreams had to do with kingdom goals like generosity with the poor and service projects for those in need. We just needed to prosper a little more first.

I decided that the best way to achieve my monetary goals was to pray this little prayer I had heard some church folk echoing in their sanctuaries. It was based on 1 Chronicles 4:10, and they were calling it the Prayer of Jabez. I only knew the gist of it to be, "Bless me, O God, and expand my territory." And because being a know-it-all was innate to my particular territory, I assumed I knew exactly what I was asking for when I beseeched for the blessing—good and happy and successful things (obviously and duh).

So I let slip from my lips those eight words a few times over, washed my hands, and thought to call it a day while I waited around for a blessing to fall from the sky. But what I didn't foresee was how that prayer would haunt me. And by *haunt* I mean that at all hours of daytime and through the night watch I found myself involuntarily motivated to echo the prayer over and over and over. There was no stopping the urge. Whenever I released those Jabez words, they would fill my belly back up and I would have to release them again and again and again:

"Bless me, O God, and expand my territory." *Prayer of Jabez*

"Bless me, O God, and expand my territory."

"Bless me, O God, and expand my territory."

At the time I couldn't have told you why this small sentence dogged my steps and kept boomeranging into my prayers. These unctions are often a mystery of the Spirit, and I think it's safe to say that the Spirit seems to go where—and move how—she pleases. In this case I think the Spirit took me at one of the words I had given her long before: *surrendered.*

For all my naivete and pride, you see, I still had enough passion for Jesus to make me burn with hunger for him. Even as a little girl I can remember my ongoing confession to God being about how I was a willing and prostrate servant, and I would go wherever/do whatever/be whoever he needed me to. So in some ways the prayer I kept praying didn't surprise me; I trusted that I was being guided somewhere valuable to our trajectory.

"Bless me, O God, and expand my territory."

The repetitive prayer was hungry, urgent, deep like oceans, and just as wet with unsolicited weeping. It rolled over my hips as I danced the words out. I stopped questioning the propelling and just kept supplicating, the plea going out from my lungs. Seemingly, my existence hung on it.

"Bless me, O God, and expand my territory."

What I couldn't have known was that my redundant recitation of those few words was an actual invitation for Someone to mess me and my family up. It never crossed my mind that a blessing as defined by Christ's kingdom might not exclusively align with my own understanding of the word. Some might say it was just a coincidence that our whole lives fell apart alongside that certain and continuous prayer, but from this end of things I can taste the work of the holy Trinity in the unraveling of the life we were striving so hard to perfect.

What the Great Ones[1] allowed during this period began with our marriage plunging headlong into a devastating crisis and continued with our work dropping out from under us. The resulting lack of income led to the eventual foreclosure of our home and the loss of a thirty-thousand-dollar investment. Add religious disillusionment and other personal issues, plus this dark thing plus that dirty thing, and faster than anyone could say "shenanigans," we were utterly wrecked—shattered like glass dropped on concrete. Our previously storm-free lives were being tossed by a raging tempest that thrashed our souls from all sides.

I tell you, though, it was under those gale forces that the Spirit guided me back to Matthew 5, where the Jesus to whom I still managed to cling told his followers that they would discover themselves blessed when they were at the end of their ropes, when they'd lost everything dear to them, when they were persecuted and put down or thrown out. That with less of them and their stuff, there would be more of God and his embrace.

I read those words and pictured myself with a backpack-load of our weighty circumstances being transported to that old hillside where Jesus sat with a ring of his followers.

His eyes are on me while I search for a seat, but the only space I want is the empty square at his feet. "May I lie down at your feet, O Truth-Speaker? Am I close enough here to know you better? I'm watching your mouth move and listening to the words you tell in that deep rumble of yours, and what you say goes against most established understandings of every time period, including mine. Teach me. Unwarp my way of thinking. Carve new pathways in my brain. How can a person be blessed when she feels tortured and nailed, crushed like an eggshell and poured out empty? I mean, everything we thought we held dear has fallen to pieces around us, and from my perspective it doesn't feel like a blessing. It feels like we're parch-throated and scaly-skinned, clawing our way through life on our hands and knees in boiling hot desert sand."

I read the passage again and again as if I sat next to the calloused knees of Jesus. Then I read it again out loud to my husband, Austin, and there on the couch, the front-row seats of our high-seas affliction, we examined our lives in light of the Matthew 5 sentences I had just read. I remember how important it felt that I turned the lights off after the reading and examining so the room could go as black as we felt. We were broken from circumstances, broken from the crushing and gnawing against our powdery pilgrim bones.

"Bless me, O God, and expand my territory" had left us a bit mangled and groping blindly in the dark with the cry on our cheeks and the grinding in our guts. I remember how we melted into the cushions and used the last bit of energy to turn two palms each toward the ceiling, our way of raising a white flag of surrender. We were so cracked that our souls were spilling out from our skin, and maybe that is why we could hear so well that night, because piercing through the black room like a shard of daylight were the words:

All this breaking is heaven's light shining on you because I want you to really know me.

Stop.

All the unbearable things were heaven's light shining on us?

Stop again.

Then I remembered the way Jesus got busted up on the way to cross, how the whole sky went dark to watch his flesh fracture, then it turned to heaven's light again on the third day when he got put back together whole for the sake and salvation of the world.

We had been whispered to by Spirit-speak that heaven's gentle light was shining on us, and for the first time in a long time, I could see it. We both could see it, the pearly rays breaking through the raging storm clouds, and we latched onto and received that truth like famished folk at a banquet feast. We needed to know that there was purpose in our pain, that the Maker was on the move in our suffering. In a rush of finality we knew the joy of having nothing left. We were peeled and raw and reeling from the blessing of dangling from the frayed edges of one last Rope, only to find it was the sure and solid hand of God gripping our slipping fingers.

"You're all we have left" came out like an abandoned sigh, and we utterly meant it when we said it.

He truly was all we had left in that moment, and the reason for the repetitious "Bless me, O God, and expand my territory" became crystal clear. He was expanding our territory to include both realities—our own "laws" and his fulfillment of them. He was giving us the means and ability to filter our entire lives differently, showing us that we had built whole value systems and formulas of thinking on a decaying platform. It—and we— needed to crumble so he could help us remake ourselves on a stronger foundation. If everything hadn't fallen apart, nothing could have been put back together.

A new, crossed-over definition of *blessing* was born in our hearts that night alongside the one already there. We didn't get the blessing I thought we would receive when I prayed that prayer like our lives depended on it, but we got the blessing that our true lives depended on. We got exactly what I had prayed for. God took me at my word that I wanted us to be blessed and our territory to expand. He just did it on his terms and not mine. What he wanted to instill in our souls was the power and surprise of an alternative, opposite, backwards, seemingly ridiculous, upside-down, desystemized kingdom.

Blessed, we learned, wasn't a word we could understand by looking it up in the dictionary or reading about it in a book or watching how society strives to define it. Blessed, as Jesus illustrates it, is a quality earned while carrying a cross over our backs in the school of hard-knock living. The world says that *blessed* means wealth and happiness; Jesus says it can mean you've got nothing left but him. The world says this and it isn't wrong, but Jesus says that and he makes everything more right.

Our family's disastrous state of affairs began to resolve itself inside our new paradigm. Our ills didn't get fixed overnight, but seeing them as a divinely appointed apprenticeship to Jesus rather than just terrible choices and circumstances allowed us to engage differently with our griefs, intentionally seek redemption, and even celebrate the joy of being gifted with these paradigm-shifting experiences. Not a blessed thing was ever the same again—including the way I looked at words I thought I knew.

On the heels of my "bless" revolution, I started chasing the tail of every other commonplace term I could think of—*love, joy, work, music, sweat, success, blood, beauty, family, mother, daughter,* everything. I chased their tails and lassoed them in to look at them with this new, opposite lens. I made them walk with me to the other side of Jesus so I could understand them again for the first time. And one after another I watched them cross over to a new, richer, profoundly meaningful place.

Why am I telling you all this? Because I hope you will try it too—to look at what you think you know and let the Spirit and your God-given imagination take you beyond it. By subverting the standardized way of seeing things, you can enjoy the possibilities of taking everyday, ordinary, already-defined words and ideas and crossing them over to the other side of Jesus. Each section of this book will focus on words that I purposefully crossed over in order to unfold in front of you what I believe their larger definitions to be. So let's go with Jesus and his stretching, redefining, ridiculous, and opposite-making ways.

The process of crossing over these words and ideas will probably require some expansion. You'll have to intentionally lay down what you think you know about something so that you can discover and receive the counterpart comprehension of it. But I'm here to tell you the sacrifice is worth it. I'm inviting you to join me in babelike wonder as a whole new wor[l]d order unfolds in front of our faces. Watch all the things get every which way more awesome.

And lastly, many people think the verses that revolutionized my concept of blessing—the Bible's Beatitudes—were taught to a huge crowd. But Matthew 5 describes that scene quite differently:

> When Jesus saw his ministry drawing huge crowds, he climbed a hillside. Those who were apprenticed to him, the committed, climbed with him. Arriving at a quiet place, he sat down and taught his climbing companions. (vv. 1–2)

[handwritten margin note: Matthew 5 was teaching his companions not a crowd?]

At the summit of that hillside in Galilee, to the few who had stuck with him, the ones winded and dripping sweat from the struggle up under the Middle Eastern heat, he delivered the most legendary message in recorded history. The Sermon on the Mount. To the ones who scaled the height, he taught the mystery. And I wonder how purposed that long hike was on Jesus' part? *Oh, I'll give you the keys to my kingdom, but you're gonna have to climb this here mountain to get them.* A little muscle-building, a little sweat-making, a little lung-stretching, a whole lot of self-sacrifice. And then . . . the view that makes it all worthwhile.

But does it?

Is a crossed-over worldview worth the cost?

Why don't you come with me and we'll see? Tie on your trekking shoes and grab your walking stick because we have some mountain-scaling to do. We can hold hands up the hill and help each other if we land on our backsides a time or two or five dozen. We are the committed secret-seekers, the climbing companions to the cross—glory be. Let's ascend the heights to trail behind his audaciously different feet.

I'm certain we'll encounter some boulders and rough terrains unknown. Based on the heaviness in my leg muscles, I can tell you that I'm also certain this is the hard-won way to getting our minds and hearts open toward a truer, bigger, new wor[l]d, kingdom dictionary.

Are you ready?

Avant-Garde

2

REDEFINING AVANT-GARDE

In July of 2000, when Austin and I got married, I was the ripe old age of nineteen and he was a seasoned twenty-four. Six months later I found out there was a baby in my belly, not on purpose. Then shortly after, another baby got in my belly not on purpose; then even less shortly after *another* baby got in my belly not on purpose.

Now, I know what you're probably thinking: somebody needs to check the date on her birth control. But I promise you that nothing short of a medieval chastity belt with a rusted-shut lock could keep this Fertile Myrtle from getting pregnant. I don't even trust the vasectomy my . . . never mind, I digress.

When our last boy was born in the left leg of my husband's pajama pants (I should probably mention I was wearing them) while we rode the elevator up to the labor and delivery floor of Yale–New Haven Hospital, I had just birthed my third baby in three years. I'll go ahead and do the math for you. I was twenty-three years young with a three-year-old wrapped around my thighs, a sixteen-month-old in one arm, a newborn in the other, and a godforsaken look of "Help!" writ across my face.

It was about this time that, as mentioned in the previous chapter, our marriage dove headlong into mess, we lost our income for too long to hang onto our home, and we experienced religious restlessness and a whole heap of other life challenges. Those early years redefined my own terms for what it meant to be drowning in the lifeblood leaking from every pore on my body. My internal equipment just wasn't mature and qualified enough for my external reality, a reality that was demanding more of me than I could bear

I could take this story in two thousand different directions from here, but the thread most befitting for this chapter starts with something that happened inside of me during those drowning days. Some psychologists call it an identity crisis, a term coined in the early 1950s by Erik Erikson to refer to a state of confusion and unhappiness over one's sense of self. That was me back then. If anyone had thought to ask me "Who are you?" in my good and lucid moments—which were few and far between—I could've answered with just about nothing. In other words, I knew maybe .02 percent of who I was.

I don't know if you've ever felt the pain of not knowing who you are or if you feel that pain right now, but what can easily happen in that place of ache is that you start looking at other people, extracting the qualities you like about them, and injecting other people's qualities into your person as a substitute for what you don't understand about yourself.

That was me too. In my naivete, I saw the people around me as more inherently gifted than I was, so I decided that self-fulfillment meant adopting their God-given gifts as my own. I looked at this person's way of socializing and that person's version of hospitality and another person's artistic expression and

We mimic others so much that we get to the point of not even knowing who we are, who God created us to be.

began mimicking their nuances. Before I knew any better, I had squeezed my shape into several different ill-fitting molds at once, while cramming my own personhood into a tiny, overlooked corner in the nether regions of my body.

What I didn't realize at the time was how devastated my spirit would become under the influence of everyone else's borrowed qualities. Other people's gifts and character traits are designed to enhance, enrich, and complement our own, but never to substitute for them. I did substitute, and the result was one damaged, frayed-looking lady.

A healthy sense of self-identity seemed to be a luxury I didn't have the currency for until three of our good friends and mentors invited us into a spiritual formation course they were offering to our community of faith. They described it as an intensive program designed to unfurl our identity, and though we didn't dissect all the details before signing up, it sounded like oxygen for us airless folk. My husband was in a similar crisis space as myself, and I knew that if we didn't do something—anything—we would surely die down inside to diddly-squat. So, along with twenty of our most trusted friends, we said yes to a year of self-discovery and the desperate hope of being born again—again.

That program turned out to be the hand of the Holy Ghost guiding us to the inner sanctums of who we were knit together to be, starting with the very first exercise on the very first day: "Draw a logo that represents who you are." But I couldn't sense that guidance at first. Because while everyone in the room seemed to be furiously making their personhood designs, I sat there in front of a piece of paper as blank as my mind. How could I draw a logo that represents who I was when I saw nothing but a vortex of nothingness inside? With that defeated thought, my tears erupted. Weeping was my only speech for those years of knowing less than an atom about which way was the up of me.

That was just the beginning. Two days a month for the ten months following, we all went through one hulk of a wringer. The facilitators were relentless with our souls, asking questions and telling stories and sharing media designed to excavate our guts. And every one of us ended up placing our disheveled, asunder insides on the table for the group to see, to poke at and pick through, and to unravel the tangled tapestries of who we were. The systems we'd bought into, the human-made rules we followed, our hidden and obvious persuaders from family, church, society, geography, and everything in between—our identities and worldviews—became clear under the light of communal analysis and reflection.

It was an out-of-our-control, suffering sort of process. But on the other side I finally got the beginnings of a grip on the whys and whos and whats of the inherent, gifted, avant-garde me.

In light of what I just shared, let me ask you some questions.

No — Do you know who you are beyond the barest bones of recognition?

Have you unraveled and examined the threads of your intimate details, or do you feel lost inside the chasm of society-induced sameness?

Do you consider conformity to be a mandate of your particular faith tradition?

Do you believe that uniqueness and creativity live within you? *Yes*

*

I imagine that we have our hands around warm cups of coffee or tea now, that we're communing face-to-face and like it matters. And this is the part where I can't help but bend a little closer because I'd like to invite you to explore one of my favorite words.

That special word is *avant-garde.*

I love the way these particular syllables roll and release and make vibrations through my vocal cords. But more than that, I love the sense of freedom and gutsy feelings they evoke.

When I first heard *avant-garde* spoken aloud, I was watching season 1 of *Project Runway*, a fashion-design reality TV show on the Bravo network. On each episode of this show, the contestants were given a unique design challenge, and the resulting creations were then flaunted on a runway to be judged. For one particular installment, the challenge was to sew something "avant-garde." And what came down the runway as a result of that challenge were some of the most absurd and outrageous outfits I'd ever seen. I loved each one. I am drawn to things that lean toward irregularity with a side of quirk and craze. After watching the show that night, I knew that *avant-garde* was a term meant for me.

Curious about the fullness of its definition, I opened dictionary .com and various other websites and began reading everything I could about *avant-garde*. And what I learned that day still haunts me.

According to my research, *avant-garde* refers to lifestyle values that are informed by unorthodox and experimental methods, daring approaches, radical pioneering, and a push against the boundaries of what is accepted as the norm or status quo. Historically *avant-garde* has been used to describe various artists, writers, composers, and thinkers whose radically creative work challenged mainstream cultural values, their only common denominator being their nonconformist approach and their desire to undermine what they see as false realities that the majority of people live shackled to. Men and women who exhibit and hold values of an avant-garde nature, who take countercultural action and subvert the normal way of seeing and doing, are sometimes referred to as vanguardists. (*Avant-garde* is simply the French word for the English word *vanguard*, referring to the front ranks of an army or a movement.)

Do any particular historical or present-day figures come to mind and strike you as avant-garde movers, shakers, reformers, or thinkers? I wish I could lie and say that the figure of Lady Gaga wasn't the first person to cross my brain space when I was trying to imagine present-day vanguardists.

I had never really been an avid follower of that particular entertainer, and she and I definitely navigate according to different moral and belief compasses. But after I spent some time examining her high-heeled eccentricities (and squirming a little as a result), I came to appreciate her willingness to hurtle herself off the cliff marked normal and fly freely into nonconformist waters. By doing so, she defined her mission, making her audience of "monsters"—aka freaks, misfits, clowns, casualties, and castoffs—believe they were wholly accepted for who they were, even though society would say they were somehow, someway, maybe all over offensive. (This might be a good and important place to annotate that one doesn't have to agree with the ideals or methods of every avant-garde figure in order to grasp their significance.)

The second person who came to my thinking space as avant-garde was Dr. Martin Luther King Jr. For most of us, MLK is a much more palatable avant-garde pill to swallow because, as sometimes happens, his ideas and influence have become mainstream. But to many in his day, Dr. King's dreams and his drive to achieve radical social reform were more "out there" and challenging than Lady Gaga's meat bikini would ever be. His words and actions changed the course of our nation and even the world.

With their unconventional habits and attitudes, both avant-garde examples agitated society and challenged the status quo. But to me the most noteworthy quality in both Gaga and Dr. King is their common denominator of fearlessness. Whether it's considerable commitment to their causes or the deepest possible desire to be different, fear is overruled so vanguardists can be who they were born to be, even at the risk of having normal society misunderstand their messages.

Avant-garde is usually used today in the context of art and music and, yes, fashion design. It applies mostly to those artsy types who live in nonconforming, counter-conventional ways. And how you respond to the word and its common manifestations might be different from how I respond. You might not naturally be drawn to the quirky and the odd. But I'd like you to pay close attention for a moment because, no matter where you're coming from, the following sentence could inform the future of who you are:

I'm certain that avant-garde is first a God-thought, a God-design, and a God-destiny for all—emphasis on all—humankind, not just a select extra-creative or extra-bold or extra-fearless few.

We were inherently designed with avant-garde identities, designed to live and move and have our unique beings within the scope of an infinitely creative God. And if an infinitely creative God is not going to run out of the stuff he's inherent in, then it follows that there should be no limit to how we creatively be and are and do, even if what we choose to be and do and are strikes those around us as strange or even threatening. If *avant-garde* refers to unorthodox lifestyles or daring thoughts or lives of radical pioneering and pushing against the status quo, then I believe the kingdom of Christ needs people with an avant-garde approach to life—including the ways in which we express our faith and spirituality.

Why do we need this approach? Because in the kingdom of humanity, vanguardists are merely an outside group of uniquely daring people who push boundaries and buck prevailing culture. But on the other side of Jesus, avant-garde identity is everyone's birthright, a divine gift from the Creator to the created. Because of that fact, no matter how your molecules are knit together in the spectrum of quiet to loud, bold to subversive, and so on, you're commissioned and permissioned to arrive at life as your own weird and wonderful self.

A kingdom vanguardist won't simply accept the status quo, either within the walls of our faith tradition or in the great earth-wide cathedral beyond bricks and mortar. Kingdom vanguardists are unorthodox, nonconformist, experimental, daring—radical pioneers of thought, value, lifestyle, art, and more. And we do it not to set ourselves apart from the rest of humanity but rather to offer an audacious and attractive invitation to the world. We are designed to be so free in our expression of true self that people who encounter us will hunger and thirst for the same kind of liberty in articulating life and making art.

Do you see why the kingdom of Christ needs people with an avant-garde approach to life? The world is dying to know a truth that will unbind, unwind, and let loose to set them free.

You will not find a better icon or rubric for avant-garde activity than Jesus. He is the original Vanguardist, eternally compromising the world's definition of normal with the first tiny cry from his universe-forming infant-lips. He was the carpenter's son who was hailed as a king, a king who looked more like a hobo gone wrong than royalty gone right. Jesus embodied the ideals of avant-garde; he was and is and is to come a figure

representing the unflinchingly unorthodox, the perfectly paranormal, the best breacher of built-up boundaries.

He wrecked whole worldviews, for instance, with his famous
"you have heard it said" statements from Matthew 5 (I'm para-
phrasing them here):

> You have heard it said, "Don't go to bed with someone else's
> spouse." But I tell you, "Don't corrupt your heart with lust."
> (vv. 27–28)
>
> You have heard it said, "Take an eye for an eye." But I tell
> you, "Don't hit back at all." (v. 38)
>
> You have heard it said, "Love your neighbor." But I tell
> you, "Love your enemy too." (v. 43)

And Jesus' actions were just as revolutionary as his words. He
seems to have committed several acts of impropriety by making
important talk with a Samaritan woman—a person who, according to Jewish law, Jesus shouldn't have even shared the same
breathing space with. He further flouted the religious conven-
tions of his time by giving valued emphasis to slaves and women,
touching the untouchable skin of lepers, healing broken bodies
on the Sabbath day, enfolding outcasts, and taking notice of the
obscure, the plain, and the little.

Because he was living out the infinitely creative essence of
God, Jesus was able to avant-garde just about everything. And
in the ultimate act of avant-garde, he paid for sins he didn't
commit.

He did none of it for the sake of fame or prestige or the
earth's idea of power or even, as some earthly vanguardists do,
just to be different. He did it all to pull the one true kingdom
into our lives right now, to liberate humankind from living in
bondage to the systems of themselves and this world.

Avant-garde as defined by Jesus liberates us from conformity, liberates us to be who we were created to be, liberates us from shaping our souls to fit society-shaped casts. Jesus still wants to save us from the suffocating bondage of the systems and traditions humans have created. He gives us permission to be unorthodox, to pioneer, to experiment, to push against the boundaries of the norm. And not just permission. As followers of Jesus, I believe we are absolutely called to unbind the chains of the status quo and approach life with an entirely new creative lens, igniting an avant-garde movement within our hearts, within our homes, within the church, within our justice projects, within our art-making, within our friendships . . . within each atom of existence.

God is infinitely diverse in his manifestations and infinitely creative in his works. But somehow, over time, we've standardized normal and prioritized status quo—rewarding crowd mentality over individuality. This is sadly and especially evident in our Christian faith tradition, which has become more about piling on formulas to follow rather than walking in the paranormal footsteps of a certain avant-garde figure named Jesus.

This prompts me to ask why so many in the church seem threatened by the new, the different, the diverse. What are we afraid of? Do we believe the divine is somehow diminished by nonconformity?

When I make a sweeping scan of the church, diversity seems to be something feared rather than something divinely mandated and celebrated. We've lost (or never fully found) a grip on the reality that each of us is born with free and independent, uniquely expressive, avant-garde identities. By its very nature, identity is avant-garde—eight billion times over. But as we grow we are too often brainwashed into thinking that sameness is the ideal. So avant-garde became a necessary response to a society who got it in their heads to make normal an ideal achievement.

Do you know what I mean? We've adapted. Conformity is learned. From the day of birth we're dropped into a vortex of patterns and systems, traditions and institutions that have been spinning for hundreds and sometimes thousands of years, our individuality and creativity barely standing a chance against the current. We are invested so heavily in this system over here and that tradition over there that many of us have less than pennies left of our true selves. We have very little room to explore our individuality because these systems and traditions and institutions mask reality, and we are deceived into thinking our true selves are fulfilled in them. (Note: individuality/identity is what we are born with before we enter the world. How that individuality is nuanced in life is largely determined by the forces around us, i.e., systems, traditions, religion, culture, geography, socioeconomic status, race, family, etc.)

Consider the system that urges us to step on the scale and scrutinize ourselves in front of the mirror. This system tells us that our worth is measured by our externals, which need to fit within society's parameters before we're accepted.

How about the age-old tradition of keeping up with the Joneses? This one keeps us spinning and striving to the fruitless end of measuring up to our neighbors.

Or how about the way educational institutions tell us that a person does not contribute value without higher schooling?

There was a time when I estimated that before the cock crowed every morning, before I had a chance to even roll off the mattress, I had already given about 10 percent of myself to the human-made systems of beauty and fashion and 10 percent to the systems of fear and 35 percent to the systems of consumerism and capitalism and 15 percent to the systems of tradition and religion and 5 percent to the systems of politics and 6 to 50 percent to the systems of "normal" and "progress" and "productivity" and "success." Sometimes the percentages would ebb and flow or give and take, and with that being the case, what did I even have left? At the beginning of each day and before my feet hit the floorboards, what percentage of my real soul or energetic real estate did I really have left to lend to my personal, indigenous, quintessential life, the avant-garde life I was actually and divinely made for?

Pause here and ponder this:

What widespread societal systems do you feel you're contracted to?

How do these systems stuff down or stifle your individuality?

I've told you why I think it's important to live out your unique nature in an avant-garde fashion. Now I'm going to tell you something even more important than comprehending your own identity. Participating in that spiritual-formation course years ago with twenty of my fellow intimates allowed me to understand my true avant-garde self in the context of the collective dynamic, and that is the most vital, pulsing part of this public-service announcement. Not only did that group experience give me vision for where I began and where I ended—my specific place in the wild and worldwide interlocking circle of contribution that represents the body of Christ. It also showed me for the very first time that where I ended, someone else began.

<u>Where I end, someone else begins.</u>

In other words, where my totally unique, avant-garde identity leaves off, someone else's totally unique, avant-garde identity starts. And I wonder if you can see in your imagination what that looks like: the whole world standing shoulder-to-shoulder, each of us representing nothing more and nothing less than the width of our singular selves? If our identities are not avant-garde at some level, then we won't be taking the place we were designed to occupy as part of the body.

I'll go ahead and say that another way: if we conform to one another's trends or embrace the general status quo rather than live out our individual, God-destined identities, we rob the body of its parts and drain the body of wholeness. We deny the body of Christ's avant-garde image that, en masse, we were always meant to represent.

Now, I'm not sure who you are, where you've come from, or where you are going, how much you fathom your distinctiveness or don't. But I do know for certain that there is only one of you, and I'm wondering if you've ever asked yourself the questions of "Where do I begin? And where do I end? What does my avant-garde personhood look like?" Because if you can't perceive the distinctive here-to-here of who you are, you'll be in danger of suffocating under the weight of comparison and covetousness and lies like "I'm not good enough, talented enough, smart enough, handsome enough . . . enough . . . enough!" Such thoughts may either be cultivated deliberately or manifested unconsciously. Either way, the kingdom of God doesn't recognize them.

Instead of listening to the banal and blasting voices of mass culture, lean in again for a moment and look into my eyes so I can tell you clear and true once more: there is only one of you. And we, your brothers and sisters of this world and the next, cannot afford to be without your real presence and your real gifts bringing fullness to our body and planting heaven in the here and now. Whatever the cost, finding the flavors of your soul and skin and speech is infinitely worth it, even if it involves challenging the system.

There's no formula or handbook for such a singular and synergistic process, but it might help for you to take along the principles of avant-garde (radically pioneer! don't conform! embrace the unorthodox! reject status quo!) when you go spelunking into the caves and crannies of your soul. Don't look to the right or to the left for a little while. Pray on your face if you need to really see yourself. Cry from your guts, ask God the questions you are burning with, and listen with all your ears and your eyes too. Be prepared to feel at times like you're being crucified on the way to your own resurrection—and try to keep your eyes on the end result. But most of all the important things, look to the One who said "I am" over and over so you would know who he is. He has already sent you a Friend in the form of his Spirit to help you know who you are.

And if you're over there knowing who you are, and I'm over here knowing who I am, and Bob is up there knowing who he is, and Bob's uncle is over yonder knowing who he is, then I'm thinking that, arm to arm united, we can make our "I am" statements and see the picture of Christ's whole body come into focus—not just ears and eyes and elbows, but stars and suns and shepherds, liberty and life and beauty and beyond.

The kingdom isn't whole until you are your one and only and always-avant-garde you.

3

[RE]LEARNING TO DANCE

A few years back our family partook in a high and holy ceremony when two of our dear friends made their marriage vows under an ancient sprawled-out tree at a Lancaster, Pennsylvania, winery. The sun was descending at just the right time for the rays to break through and shine between all the branches, twisted arms of great-grandfather wood backlit with shimmering shafts of solar light. There were jars of petaled bouquets hung suspended on iron hooks next to rows of stark white chairs, and nature showed us her colors in a panorama of degrees and depths—rolling hills, vibrant landscape, infused air (show-off!). The whole scene was afire with fragrance and glory and heaven bursting onto earth's scene.

After our friends' pledging sacrament, we celebrated here on terra firma the way we imagined God and all the angels were partying on the other side of the visible world: we danced like cuckoos with an extra side of crazy. And by *cuckoos* and *crazy* I mean that our very skin and limbs seemed to come unhinged and move as if no mind controlled them at all, as though our bodies were rubberized extensions of our souls, as though we were mostly outside of our beings while fully inviting all the burn in our muscles and the sweat on our flesh. We laughed and lost our breath and depleted our energy to the nth amount, hallelujah! Dancing is my favorite way to rejoice in the entire occupied universe.

But even better than embodying the sensations of total, artless liberty was watching our three boys and their from-birth buddies cut themselves loose on the boogie floor. They didn't quit for two full hours. And after the dancing was done, our second son, Seth, came to my ears and spoke excitedly, with a beginner's quality of disbelief: "Me and Eli kept wanting to take a break, but then another good song would come on and we just couldn't stop dancing!"

Ahh! My mama face couldn't stop stretching with smiles at that, just as I'd smiled while watching their totally free motion of stems flying outward, spirits soaring upward.

What I want you to know especially, though, is what my friend Brie told me about Seth's dancing. Halfway through the song list, Brie had slid up next to Seth while he was grooving and asked him, "Where did you get all your awesome dance moves?"

And without pausing to think or missing a foot-stomping step he'd replied, "I was born with them."

✳

In Richard Rohr's book *Falling Upward,* I read a researched commentary about newborn babes and how they see themselves completely mirrored in their mother's or father's gaze, how they know themselves in the security provided by those who hold them and look into their eyes with love. If a baby is looked at well and true, then that first sense of contact and kinship begins the uniting consciousness to which they will always and ultimately want to come back to.

This uniting consciousness is the embrace of what Rohr terms the "Great Divine Gaze," and babies know intrinsically that they can make no wrong move within its power. "Like any true mirror, the gaze of God receives us exactly as we are, without judgment or distortion, subtraction or addition. Such *perfect receiving* is what transforms us."[1]

As long as children are held fully within the gaze of love, you never have to teach them how to express themselves freely and without fear. They are perfectly unself-conscious until they are met with the glaring eyeballs of the world outside that first stare of love; only then will a child begin to lose the confidence of all-encompassing love and—consequentially—the birthright of the inherent, avant-garde expressiveness instilled in us all from the moment of Creation.

I've read the biblical story of Adam and Eve in the garden many times, and I am admittedly no theologian when it comes to parsing out the interpretations and semantics of Scripture. Some people say the whole kit and kaboodle of the narrative is metaphor. Other people believe it's through and through exactly literal. I probably land somewhere in the grey space between the two. But all that aside, I can see this gaze-truth Richard Rohr speaks of mirrored there between the trees.

Young and tender like newborn babes, with bald feet and bare flesh, Adam and Eve traversed the earth in the safety and spirit of utopian love. They "were naked, but they felt no shame."[2] They had nothing added to their insides and nothing added to their outsides; it was just their DNA mixed with divinity. They didn't even know the state of their starkness because they were wrapped within the purity of perfect affection—until one infamous serpent spoke seductively to the woman and drew her eyes away from the only gaze that would reflect back her true, totally embraced self.

"Do I understand that God told you not to eat from any tree in the garden?" murmured the serpent. And the woman, with curiosity in her composition, made her first mistake. She diverted her eyes from the gaze.

"Not at all," she responded to that slithering symbol of seduction. "We can eat from the trees in the garden. It's only about the tree in the middle of the garden that God said, 'Don't eat from it; don't even touch it or you'll die.'"

But the serpent responded with sneak in his speak, assuring the woman, "You won't die. God knows that the moment you eat from that tree, you'll see what's really going on." And the Eve-lady, new as a baby, fell for the lie, not understanding that God had spoken to her the express truth. Death would indeed result from such an unfortunate bite—the death of her innocence, a far deeper demise than any bodily dying.

Eve ate the death-making fruit. Her mate followed suit. And immediately following the swallowing, our Adam and Eve did see what was really going on—they realized they were naked! They saw their nakedness as a shameful thing because it revealed how they had invited something else and ugly into their divine and DNA mix.

Deceit slithered along and spoke in the garden and drew the eyes of those first children away from the Parent-gaze, the gaze that had guarded them entirely and reflected back their honest, love-consumed beings. As a result, innocence was extracted from the marrow of their baby-like bones and replaced with a worldly, all-grown-up knowledge.

What died that day was the dance moves they had made

without even thinking, the "I was born with them" beauty of their natures, their unaffected, innocent selves.

After that, when they heard the sound of their Parent strolling in the garden's evening breeze, the ashamed and afraid Adam and Eve camouflaged themselves among the vegetation until God opened his mouth and spoke: "Where are you?" This was no guileless game of hide-and-go-seek.

"Where are you?" he asked because the true selves of these children he loved had gone missing. I suspect that, more than being angry, his heart was broken in jagged halves.

"I heard you in the garden and I was afraid because I was naked," said the man. I can imagine and sympathize with Adam's fear, the great collision of frightening feelings happening in his unaccustomed body. But my heart extends even further to the Parent as he responds to his child with a sentence more split with pain than all the other words of the ancient Old Testament books.

"Who told you you were naked?" the Maker asked. And his insides hemorrhaged with the hurt of a million mustangs stampeding on his heart. The veins grew hot in his neck and the trembles there were not cool, calm, or collected.

"Who told you you were naked?"

(Who told you that you weren't enough? That you were ugly? That you weren't smart? That you couldn't dance? That you weren't creative? That you were boring? That you weren't original?)

"Who told you you were naked?"

And the Parent made some disciplinary decrees to his first-born children—banishment and curses and toil. But the very next instant he turned himself Tailor and "made leather clothing for Adam and his wife and dressed them."

Can't you see it? Stitch by painstaking stitch the Tailor sutures the hides together with the ribbons of one very injured aorta. His weeping is a waterfall, dripping down his chin and dropping on his devastated, darning hands. And from the crack of his devastated voice still come the words: "Who told you you were naked? . . . (stitch) . . . Who told you you were naked? . . . (stitch) . . . Who told you you were naked? . . . (stitch) . . . Who told you you were naked? . . . (stitch) . . . Who told you . . ."

Which is the suffering equivalent of: "Where are you?"

And "Where are the moves I made you with?"

Stepping outside the gaze results in an absolute crumbling of one cosmic heart and an apocalypse to the human soul.

In his world-renowned TED talk, creativity expert Sir Ken Robinson says that "children dance all the time if they're allowed to," which has led me to believe that every child is born a dancer, but the hard hammerings of the world tend to train and drain the rhythmic pattern of steps out of the little ones as they get older. I personally know this axiom to be true because my mama says I was an unself-conscious dancer in my toddler days, shaking my diapered booty to any bit of music that came across the airwaves. But what she and I can't recall is exactly when time and circumstances caused me to stop the innocence of my unaffected moves.

Somewhere along the way, I turned my neck and shifted my eyes from the total love of the divine reflected in my parents' gaze, allowed myself to be informed by people and patterns that didn't love me completely, and therefore, on this earth, I stopped dancing. I feared that I wasn't doing it right and wondered what other people thought of my moves and felt judged and embarrassed if I danced my feet the "wrong" way.

By the time I reached twenty, my flesh felt like it was harboring more than a decade of stacked up, stored, and locked-tight movement in its stationary appendages. I still remember how my whole body burned for motion when watching people who could fly around a dance space without restraint. Why couldn't I let go and be free like that? There was an ache way down to the interior abyss of my soul, an ache that was begging for me to have just enough liberty to let go a little. But because I didn't know who I was, how to express myself, or how much I was loved, my body was bound inflexible with a fear that if I moved myself freely in front of people, I would look stupid in every possible way.

Dancing, of course, is just an analogy for the avant-garde, childlike soul we are all gifted with. And my story is everyone's story and represents the truth that we've all experienced—some version of losing the innocent, unsuppressed expression of our truest selves.

We've all lost something of what we were born with; we have all felt a measure of pain at being cramped into shapes and structures that don't define us or fit us or release us. And the question you might be asking here is: "How does anyone get to the place where they feel beautiful and confident in their own skin, in their own style, in their special expressions and gifts, in their own unique wholeness?"

"How do I get back the moves I was born with?"

In his book *The God-Shaped Brain,* psychiatrist Timothy R. Jennings suggests a possibility. He references a research study that revealed that contemplatively meditating on the love of God has a more healing influence on the brain than any other practice or effort we put forth in order to reach identity integrity and abandon.[3]

In short, we get our inherent dancing moves back and find the freedom of our uniqueness when we actively return to the gaze again and again. Getting consistently caught in the look of love liberates us from the onslaught of the oppressive and binding lies and systems we've listened to, organically making room for us to bloom from the inside out.

Throughout the process of my own healing, I can confidently say that the persistent hours I spent lying flat-out on the floorboards of my living room with tears and silence and nothing in my mind except the eyes of God looking at me with love—meditating on his adoration until I understood just a small measure more of it—restored a greater sense of my true self than any other practice (retreats, workshops, books, exercises) I've tried.

Do try this at home because contemplative "sits" with a loving God can be the key ingredient to your free unfurling.

We spend so much time today mimicking what Eve did in the garden—eating the forbidden fruit and losing ourselves to snakes and systems and lies—that I'm wondering now what kinds of things you've bargained away?

What is suffocating or shackling your precious and only self?

What would it look like for you to begin reimagining your own unique moves?

Do you know how important it is for you to get your groove back?

Richard Rohr says that "your essence, your exact 'thisness,' will never appear again in another incarnation."[4] And if that isn't reason enough to labor toward knowing the most emancipated form of yourself, then think about this: our true selves with all their singular, cherished, irreplaceable nuances and distinctions and subtleties are a hazard to the human-made empires we've constructed (praise God) and an anchor to the economy of heaven being brought down to earth. If we're going to dismantle that which we've constructed in our own broken image—the very thing that is destroying us—and raise up instead the living, breathing, real and right kingdom come, then we each need to know our gorgeous, uncommon particulars.

I didn't start dancing again until my identity and worth were more informed by the gaze of God and less informed by the systems and rules of humankind. Finding my true self was a pilgrimage back to the garden, a return to being held in the eyes of the divine.

And now that I'm raising my own kids, I believe it isn't possible to keep our offspring within the protective parental gaze forever. I've never seen a bubble big or broad enough to keep out the rigors of reality. We don't live in Eden anymore, and the cycle of necessary suffering and crucifixion before transformation and resurrection seems to be a global code written in the fabric of the universe and a rite of passage for the secret seekers. You cannot find yourself again, it seems, if you haven't first known the ache of utter loss.

This happens over and over and over throughout the course of a life and I'm convinced that our job as parents is not to protect our kids from human experience—the double-edged sword that will cut them wide open—but to give them the tools that will help them make a resurrected return, again and again, to the brilliant allure of the divine gaze, the tools to know that any stare other than the divine gaze is not the true story and that finding themselves in the gaze is the foundation of self-knowledge.

"I was born with them," Seth says, and there is not a doubt in my mind that those are some of the truest words ever spoken. Every one of us is born with all the moves we need for unbridled dancing (and living) before the world, with its systems and boxes and rules and institutions and traditions and lies, wrings them dry or binds them up. But these systems don't have to make us afraid or keep us in their clutches. Instead, they can be seen as media available to catalyze change and learn our true, peculiar selves.

I've watched around me for a while now, and I've seen how we grow out of our inherent, avant-garde natures as we get older . . . and necessarily so. If we don't lose our inherent selves to some extent, we can never go through the arduous cocreative process of stumbling along the Calvary road at the wounded side of Jesus. On that hill our false selves are designed to die so we can be resurrected into a more accurate incarnation of true self— each time and cycle bringing us closer to the gaze that frees us up from the inside out.

This is the foundation of our relationship to the Trinity—to walk hand-in-hand, skin-to-skin. And if we don't know the pain of wondering where all our moves went, we'll never fully give our loose-limbed thanks when they return to us. The dancing and the not-dancing are counterparts, and life is a balance of opposites that must be understood and embraced side by side in order to inform the fullness of their individual meaning. In other words, you have to forget how to dance in order to fully appreciate getting your movement back.

No. We do not live in the garden anymore, and suffering is a necessary step in the direction we must go to find our true selves. But I imagine there is still weeping between the trees when we listen to the lies and rejoicing when we return to the gaze that covers us so fully in love, when we can once more be fully naked—body and soul—and not know it or not care. I imagine the ancient David—who is rumored to have flung himself around the city streets of Jerusalem in his birthday suit, rowdy in his praise and causing a ruckus of a scene—was a guy who knew he could make no wrong move within the power of the divine gaze.

The light of the Parent's gaze is the most haunting and alluring component of living I've ever experienced, always calling me forward and further. Inch by inch and time after time I am moving through my crucifixions and getting closer to who I really am. And you should see how I dance now. I dance every time like I've been inhaled by the Spirit to a paranormal place—dance like I don't own my body and yet it's entirely mine, like I'm inside myself and beyond myself. I dance like it's my job, because it is. It's my job to be a daughter held in the Parent's eyes, seeing myself reflected back with an unrelenting, undefiled love. When my limbs personify that love, the movement is transcendent.

Maybe for you it's not about dancing.

Maybe your feet move just fine, but other parts of your creative self are all clogged up or just copycat because you're too far from the gaze to see your true, peculiar, avant-garde self reflected in the Eyes of the One who gave you life.

I'm asking you now to come with me, and together we'll walk our bodies closer and closer to the radiant gaze that holds us in perfect love. The desire to rediscover our true selves, our very own avant-garde movement, is intrinsic in all human beings and imperative for fulfilling our contributions in the world. Together we're wrestling our way home to the radiant beam of universal love, which is the sum total meaning of life and how we make heaven visible to earth.

4

THE GIFT OF NOT

During my formative years I spent my Sunday mornings and Wednesday nights with a moderately conservative sect of the Christian faith tradition.

Now, because *conservative* can mean different things to different folks, what I mean is we had a worship band and tambourines and drummers stick-banging in time with songs like "Lord, I Lift Your Name on High," "Shine, Jesus, Shine," and "Awesome God," but there were no charismatic-y happenings that I can recall. And because *charismatic-y* can mean different things to different folks, what I mean is not a single person in our church did any tongue-talking or flag- throwing or dancing in the aisles or slaying brothers and sisters in the Spirit. I didn't have a clue that such experiences even existed.

In other words, I grew up in a bona fide church bubble, a bubble I loved with all the zeal of my young, passionate, Jesus-adoring heart. In my youthful estimation we had the best pastors, best programs, and best people anywhere.

Life and church went on this way until late in my seven-teenth year, when a twelve-person, college-aged traveling team from a worldwide missions organization showed up at our church to present a multimedia production for the youth group. The mobile production was designed to recruit its audience to full-time missions. To that end, the performers sang inspiring songs and acted in stimulating skits and spoke soul-stirring sermons. But for me, by far the most influencing element of the entire show was one tall, dark, and very handsome Texan.

Never in all my born days had I seen anything so beautiful with my own eyeballs. Not only did this guy have the hotness to make a girl's armpits pour forth besotted sweat, but he also played Jesus in the various sketches the team acted in. And when a gorgeous guy gets up on a stage and plays Jesus, what red-blooded, good Christian girl with any semblance of a pulse wouldn't beat an errant fist against her chest and grunt "Me want" like a Neanderthal?

Along with about fifty other girls in the auditorium that day, I fell hard for that guy—hard. The organization's recruiting maneuver (read: smoking-hot man hunk) worked especially well in my case because less than three months later I found myself transplanted to Texas, attending a discipleship course, and get-ting equipped for a life of full-time ministry. (Note: I married the guy.) And also becoming part of a decidedly charismatic-y community.

You could say that I was removed from one particular kind of Christian bubble and dropped directly into another, but this was a *very* different bubble. My previous church experience hadn't prepared me for all the flag-throwing and prayer-yelling and aisle-dancing and Spirit-slaying and such. To be honest, it looked and sounded to me like a whole circus full of clown-foolery. But I embraced the lively expression of these gospel freaks and soon found myself yearning for a specific spiritual gift—the gift of tongues.

It seemed like tongues were all around me in those days. I would watch closely as dozens of people in our prayer room worshiped with their special prayer language, and I watched as others were blessed with the gift themselves shortly after their initiation to this charismatic place. But it wasn't happening with me. I prayed all the prayers and cried all the tears and begged on needy knees, asking the Almighty to release the gift of tongues inside me. Still nothing. For the duration of my discipleship period, people would come one after the other to lay their hands on my head and pray over me. With deeply furrowed brows they would beseech the heavens on my behalf. It seemed, in their eyes, I wasn't a wholly realized Christian until I could speak in tongues.

But my—and their—best efforts did not avail. I never did get that gift, and my spirit was crushed under the assumption that something was devastatingly wrong with me or that some "sin in my life" was blocking the Spirit from loosening my vocal cords. I received advice from everyone under the scalding southern sun:

"Just let go and don't think about it."

"All you have to do is ask God and believe."

"The enemy is preventing you from getting the gift; resist him!"

And so on and so forth until, not surprising, I perceived myself to be smaller spiritually than everyone else. At times I even wondered if maybe God loved me less.

I was feeling bereft and on the outside of a special circle as this particular gift and its lack in my life became a sore subject in my spiritual experience. So I slammed the book shut and shelved it firmly and quietly in a tiny, far-reaching corner of my interior—a place where I could more easily ignore the ache and carry on with the business of feeling as equally adequate as my peers and preceptors—while harboring secret thoughts that, for some reason unbeknownst to me, I didn't fit inside the religious mold of the organization I was involved with.

I didn't know back then what I know now—that I was up against a well-intentioned but immovable system of theology that attempted to squeeze my design inside a parameter I wasn't made for. The fruit of my Christian life had become suspect not because of any defect in me, but because I couldn't perform by their book.

I've heard multiple accounts from people who share similar experiences to mine, experiences where the size and singularness of each person was actively shoved into the crate of systemized religion. My prayer-language story is just one example of how our various faith traditions try, often unwittingly, to contain and domesticate the Spirit within a methodology that stifles the uniquely creative self, tailoring a person to what a particular tradition believes a religious person should be like, forcing a person into the image of God that they themselves created.

My intention in writing this is not to cause an unhealthy, unholy, divisive uproar. (If there is to be an uproar, let it be for the good.) My heart is not to irritate or offend. But may I gently suggest that it would be a mistake to think that Christ followers are somehow immune from the insidious tendency to create systems that stifle and block the God-made self?

The hard truth is that we, the church, are often the greatest perpetrators of systematic bondage—that is, institutionalization.

Institutionalization is a way of standardizing beliefs and methods and insisting that individuals fit that mold. This practice is so prevalent in our faith tradition that we often don't even realize its effects. And sometimes I wonder, along with Frederick Buechner, that,

> maybe the best thing that could happen to the church would be for some great tidal wave of history to wash all that away— the church buildings tumbling, the church money all lost, the church bulletins blowing through the air like dead leaves, the differences between preachers and congregations all lost too. Then all we would have left is each other and Christ, which was all there was in the first place.[1]

What if all we did have was each other and Christ? I feel refreshed just imagining it because the church is nothing more or less than the people who choose to embody Christ while he's (technically) absent on the earth. But that's not what so many people experience when they get involved with Christianity.

My story is miniscule compared to far more damaging narratives of subjection I have heard—stories of men's and women's organic relationship with the Spirit being brought into an institutionalized line that must be toed in order for their faith to be considered real or approved. It's not just a charismatic thing. Or a Catholic thing. Or a nondenominational thing. Or a mainline thing.

It can happen in any religious organization. It *does* happen in every single one. Which makes me tend to agree with so many others who maintain that religion, in its various forms and functions, is a human-made system of behaviors and beliefs. Religion, basically, is what the world does. And at the risk of being redundant, I'm going to say it again almost the same way: religion is a mortal thought.

That's not to say we should go out and tear down churches.

Remember, we said from the beginning that systems aren't inherently evil. They're just not what the kingdom is about.

Remember, when the world says *this*, Jesus says *that*. And what Jesus *didn't* come to do was to establish a system of religion. He came in opposition and revolution against the systems of the world, even the religious ones, designing to take us away and way beyond doctrines and denominations and the mentality of humanity. He had no intention of establishing on earth what was already being done. Instead, he came to set the wrongs of our backward world to rights, to establish an alternative to the dispositions of society, to show us how to be fully, truly, madly, deeply alive and free. As the apostle Paul wrote in the book of Galatians:

> Is it not clear to you that to go back to that old rule-keeping, peer-pleasing religion would be an abandonment of everything personal and free in my relationship with God? I refuse to do that, to repudiate God's grace. If a living relationship with God could come by rule-keeping, then Christ died unnecessarily. (Galatians 2:21)

Jesus came to establish the kingdom of God, a kingdom that bends low and serves the world with a self-humiliating, savage, and sacrificial love. And if you come with me to Bethlehem and have yourself a squalling little baby, a baby who will dog your every waking day if you only take a single sideways look at the situation, you will find that this is not about religion.

Jesus is an original, which is why this is about a love affair and nothing less. We were made to be governed by a love so deep, so wide, so high we don't need human-made rules and systems to keep us looking perfect and pure or acting according to a single version of Christ expression.

We've added much to our love affair and need to take notice

of the stuff and nonsense we've stacked on top of our amour. Because it's the add-ons that are often the architects of uniformity and the destroyers of honest, indigenous soul expression. It's a damaging practice to tell people how to pray or how many "quiet times" to have in a week (seven, obviously) or how their daily creativity or mission should manifest or the exact words for repentance.

I know that certain systems and structures and programs within the institution of church are intentioned to create healthy parameters, maintain efficiency, and lend to the flourishing of the church. And if a system or structure is led by the Spirit, it has potential to be a good thing.

Here's how you tell the difference: If a religious system dominates or powers over you and tries to manage your behaviors or beliefs, it's a human-made system. If a system is designed to come under you and support the growth of your love with Christ and your rare, creative, contributing self—if it seeks to support the health of your heart first, not manage your behaviors or beliefs—then it's manifested from the Spirit.

What I'm addressing in this chapter is the ways in which we have systematized the Spirit, made hard rules and decided that the way he works for one person is the way he works for every person, taking the elements of awe and surprise away from his inherent nature and thereby creating a sluggish atmosphere with rote and robotic motions that numb an individual's own unique life-making. These things lead to dependence on the institution instead of on Christ.

In other words, the Christian traditions are often afflicted with a pandemic of uniformity. Many of us in it are afraid to venture outside the norm even when our whole beings ache to break prototype. We were fashioned for the blazing glory of a divergent God to be displayed within the collection of us. We were not fashioned for the whitewashed, squeaky-clean, structured and suited version of Christianity we so often see and represent. And yet we studiously maintain the box-ticking and boundary-keeping that has us all looking and thinking and speaking the same—with disastrous results, as evidenced by the sorry and shattered condition of my heart after months of being told there was something wrong with me because I couldn't talk in tongues.

Cookie-cutter spirituality doesn't work. How in the wide world of everything could it possibly do so when we're made in the image of an infinitely creative and diverse God? And when I say "infinitely creative and diverse," I'm thinking of a million different shades of skin and sixty-five hundred spoken languages and between two and fifty million species of animals and no two snowflakes alike. My friend Jim tells me that when an infinitely creative God tries to pour himself into the finite, we get a hundred thousand types of trees, each one expressing attributes of God—a weeping willow shows his vulnerability while an oak displays his sturdiness.

The apostle Paul tells us to look at nature for a display of God's invisible qualities. And this is what I see when I stretch my eyeballs over the created order: I see a God whose anthem is variety, invented and celebrated. I also see a God who invented beautiful, intricate, orderly, and mysterious systems that serve and support the universe as a whole.

See, I'm not saying all systems are bad. A system is good if it comes under, rather than powers over, the parts and people involved, if it serves rather than simply self-perpetuates. The trouble is that human-made systems, including religious organizations, often lean in overpowering directions.

Our world is weary of overused platitudes and programs, and the cure to our own banality is to actively sink deeper into the absolute nonconformist nature of the Spirit. The cure is to take two-handed and wholehearted possession of our relationship with the Author of diversity. Because if we truly understand God's avant-garde nature, it gives us permission to break free from the expectations and labels that are cramping our souls— even, maybe especially, the religious ones. It gives us permission to come alive.

As I mentioned in chapter 2, Austin and I attended a spiritual-formation course early in our marriage, and during that course I started to excavate my true identity from the fossilized caverns of my false self. Inauthentic statutes and systems, patterns, and persuaders were getting uncut and unchipped all around inside me. Bit by bit I was letting go of things I'd adopted from a misguided conformist position and learning the truth of my specific parts. Like uncaged birds, my peculiarities were making themselves free.

As that was happening, there came this singular day that changed the trajectory of my relationship with God. Not too unlike the scene in *Sleeping Beauty* where Aurora slips into a trance and is unwittingly propelled to prick her finger on a spindle, I found myself transfixed and lured by the Spirit-Wind to an empty closet in the guest bedroom of our home. I stepped into that black and quiet space and sensed that the air inside those tiny walls was somehow different—charged, the molecular mix crackling with anticipation.

I began speaking my most honest "regular" prayers, and before I could divine the doing, my arms started swinging and swaying of their own volition, seemingly in tune with the utterances coming off my mouth. I had enough wherewithal in that moment to open myself up to the movement without holding back or calling a stop to it. And sooner than I could register this reality, my limbs were moving all over the place and my face was watered with weeping.

Because time doesn't seem real in situations like this, I don't know how long I kept moving like that. I had long since stopped speaking and just let the movements pray for me. But when I was done, I knew that I knew that I knew that this occasion was the beginning of something special, mine and the Spirit's, ours alone. This was the day of my first unexplainable, metaphysical experience, and I determined afterward to show up again and see what the Holy Ghost would continue to do with me.

The next event was much the same, except I felt cramped by the small walls of the closet and decided to grant my body-prayers more room to function and flow freely. Before long the whole wide living room was my supplication station, and every last inch of me went wild with my newfound gift of body-prayer. I broke my own rules for how to create kinetics. I motioned in ways my appendages had never performed previously. Afterward I lay flat on the floor, having used myself up completely, and spilled out my emotion on the rug in gratitude at the realization that my great nonconformist God, the avant-garde God with diversity in their trinitarian bones, never intended me to have the gift of speaking in tongues because kingdom come needed and needs prayer movers and dancers too.

As this realization hit, healing was instantaneous. God had never abandoned me or deemed me unworthy of being a tongue talker. All along he had something more unconventional in mind for me, something I had never seen in the religious institutions I frequented.

Now I pray with my body more than I pray with my mouth. My limbs are a conduit of the Spirit in times when my mind can't discern what's going on behind the physical scenes. Not only does God meet me in unorthodox ways, but he also invited me to them. He invited me outside the lines of what I'd seen our faith tradition doing. He invited me to something I previously hadn't heard of or seen. He confirmed the rareness of my identity, the uniqueness of my relationship to him, and the particular offerings I present to the world.

I've been praying with my body for nine years now, throwing these limbs around like I don't own them. Not unlike people who speak in tongues, I turn to my body when my guts are wrung dry by suffering and injustice and evil. I turn to my body when I can't hold anymore the fountains of effervescent joy and praise. I turn to my body when an unidentifiable unction takes over and I have no idea what actually needs praying.

I just move—I let wordless words spill through hard or gentle, slow or fast movement, sometimes with a side of groaning and keening. These are the nonsyllables for saving my soul and letting the kingdom come. I don't always know what they are for, but I can feel heaven shaking earth every time my foot beats against the ground and my arms stretch towards the sky and my tear ducts rush like white-water rapids; when I drop and bend and surge and fall again, only to rise up higher before going low and landing on my knees, heart pumping hard like a hundred racing stallions and back arched bow-style before the aching heart of God and whatever the Great Ones ask me to steward with them.

I pray with my body, and this devoted dialect is totally ours, mine and Theirs. (Maybe it's yours too, but in a different way.) Together we make love on this earth, bringing heaven down to the floorboards and through the trees, bending branches and sweeping alongside the Wind with the power of our unity. This specific form of prayer will never be repeated under the whole always sky.

And I know I'm a crazy person, a fool for Christ's sake if ever there has been one with my utterly loosed gift of not-tongues.

What does it all mean? I don't know exactly, but I do know the Great Ones knit me together with something totally avant-garde in mind. They needed me to raise the kingdom through dance the same way that other people lift the kingdom through speech. And while I still pray words with all the ardor of my God-loving heart, nothing compares to the communion we share when we dance together.

The apostle Paul tells us: "Don't become so well-adjusted to your culture that you fit into it without even thinking. Instead, fix your attention on God" (Romans 12:2). God-gazing is the only way, the antidote to living in the trance of institutions—church and otherwise. From your rightful place inside the gaze, with your vision wide open, look around and know what you're accepting and ascribing to in your daily life. There are systems involved. Are you under their spell?

I'm writing this from my knees because these are the days for being a bit of a menace and exercising a little madness, like the turbulent prophets of old times and again the apostle Paul when he tells us that we all have different gifts in the same body (1 Corinthians 12). And I'm going to use my exhortation gift right here to tell you this: It's entirely possible that your uncommon, individual communion with the divine has been neither defined nor sanctioned by tradition. It's entirely possible that your faith, your love affair with Father, Son, and Holy Ghost, is infected with mandated ways and systems. Systems are a futile substitute for the ecstatic, run-around, wide-open field of being heirs to Christ's creativity.

Your relationship with God is uniquely, only yours—designed in the heavens to be flooded with colors unseen and awash with speechless frequencies, undected and undefined and perhaps undignified. Approach your faith with the eyes of a vanguardist and lose yourself differently, distinctly to the passions of Christ. As Paul puts it, "live freely, animated and motivated by God's Spirit" (Galatians 5:16).

Examine and identify, decide what stays and what goes, what you can live without and what you can healthily participate in. And if your relationship with God is built on ideas passed down and spoon-fed to you by the institutions of humanity, I give you permission to rub your two sticks together, stumble into a moment, and build from the ground up—starting with the naked truth of a diverse divinity and your unique self.

Is there anything keeping you from the breathtaking, exuberant chase of freedom in your relationship with God?

What are some of the systems of your specific faith tradition that are manacled to your mind, that don't allow you to organically manifest your love for God?

What do you imagine a system-extracted, avant-garde relationship with God would look like for you?

Can you even imagine it?

If you can imagine it, what does breaking free look like?

5

UNORTHODOX PARENTING

It was a Sunday afternoon in June and my heavy, sad steps carried my heavy, sad legs up the stairs to the master bedroom. For the first time in a very long while, I crawled my heavy, sad body across the mattress and curled my heavy, sad self fetal-like on the bed. I was bowled horizontal from sorrow. And by "sorrow" I mean: *For the love of all things holy, who's pulling out my intestines and stomping all over them?*

At the same time I was horizontal from sorrow, Austin was driving thirteen hours home from a North Carolina summer camp nestled in the foothills of the Blue Ridge Mountains. He had just delivered our twelve-year-old son, Gabe, to the place where he would be serving for two months straight. Austin told me later that after leaving Gabe he'd big-baby-bawled so hard that he had to pull over because his ability to drive safely was compromised.

That same boy is convinced he was born with a deep and wide spirit of adventure because while I was five months pregnant with him, I backpacked for six weeks across western Europe, visiting countless cities in nine countries total. Maybe he's right. Maybe while my legs were negotiating new lands, my womb was literally knitting the go in his toes and the hunt for adventure in his heart and the ache for unknowns within his eyes. Or maybe the great Designer knew what the world would need in a Gabriel Marcus Morrison and made him a certain way to fit that need. Maybe both.

From the time he was five months old, Gabe began displaying an acute and annoying restlessness whenever we were trying to chill at home, squawking and fussing and being a generally loud and hell-raising nuisance—adorably and endearingly so, of course. But as soon as he saw one of us carrying his car seat from the front entryway, that boy would suck his high-pitched hollering behind his gums and start flapping his excited arms like a turbo-powered albatross. He did it every single time. One of his very first words was an energized and emphatic "Go!" which he usually repeated as if he were a pull-string doll with the mechanism stuck: "Go go go go go go-go go-go go-go gooooooooo!" all day long.

For the first twelve years of his life, the most predictable words out of Gabe's mouth—after "Good morning, Mama, how did you sleep?"—were "What are we doing today?" As if new lands could be explored and conquered between every sunrise and sundown.

At eleven, Gabe started entertaining far-reaching adventuring ideas when we were studying Daniel Boone in homeschool. We learned that at the age of ten, Daniel left the hearth and arms of his immediate family to make his own way in the world. Ten! He was ten years old when he moved to the wilderness alone, single-handedly managing his father's second farm. Sitting next to Gabe during that story allowed me to hear his thinking wheels turn as we talked around this historical character and his young-age endeavors. I could practically feel the yearning as Gabe looked beseechingly and boldly at my face and verbalized his own entrenched need for a Daniel-Boone-type experience. But alas, we are several centuries removed from the 1700s. How could I facilitate his exploratory urges in modern society?

At twelve Gabe started getting more ideas in his head when our family sat down to watch a documentary film called *Maiden Trip*, the story of a fourteen-year-old Dutch girl who sailed around the world for two years by herself. As in all alone on the wide-open ocean. As in far, far, far from the land of her mom and dad. As in four years before she was technically an adult. As in were her parents crazy? But the whole time we were watching this movie, we were also registering the inherent traits and desires of this Dutch girl, and all Austin and I could really see was the myriad similarities between our son and this incredible girl.

Maybe there's a certain breed of people—like Daniel Boone and the Dutch girl and Gabe—who are built differently from us other folk. Or maybe it has equal parts to do with how they're intentionally nurtured and how they're intrinsically natured. Whatever the origin, we knew there were appetites in Gabe about to erupt, and finally the moment happened. Our big boy was only halfway past twelve when he asked if we could please find him a place where he could go away on his own for the whole summer and serve. Key need: being on his own.

Gabriel didn't fit the status quo of most twelve-year-olds. Gabe fit the unique size and shape of his intrinsic self, not some chart or tradition, and that meant he was ready to come of age before the numbers next to his name were the right digits. What he needed from us was to find him a physical experience to anchor his developing maturity.

So I Google-searched until my eyeballs dropped out and

asked everyone and everywhere until my tongue went dry. I was desperately looking for an opportunity that would come alongside the bloom of our boy. But after weeks of inquiries and for one reason or another, nothing that would remotely work for us was presenting itself.

The most common obstacle I hit was the scarcity of work/ service opportunities available for kids who are Gabe's age. "He's only twelve," I would hear. Most organizations took sixteen-year-olds and older, and no amount of sweet-talking on my part could convince anyone to bend the rules or make an exception. I had about given up when I happened to mention my woes to one more friend, who miraculously responded with: "I know people all over the country who run summer camps. I can get you in touch with them."

At my friend's insistence that she could assist in finding Gabe a summer-long experience far away, I was suddenly swamped with conflicted feelings. Our son had made it clear he needed an undertaking that would test his mettle and satiate his sky-high adventurous streak. "I just have to do this," he would say. But what did he know? Could I trust his own self-reflection and young gut instincts?

I'll admit that in a moment of weakness and uncertainty I spent a minute looking around me, measuring and analyzing other parents, and couldn't find any who were sending their young sons away for such a long time. But I quickly dismissed my comparative thoughts and went deep into conversation with my husband while we picked apart our own gut feelings. Despite what we saw being done and not being done in various families, we needed to learn what was right for our family, even if our choices seemed questionable to others. (We did get questioned.) And those choices would leave our hearts laid out on the ground, open and at risk.

In the end, we chose to release our son—but not for the sake of being different or to impulsively exercise unconventional parenting. We let him go because we were Spirit-led to engage with our own avant-garde Parent and felt permissioned by him to challenge the status quo for Gabe's benefit. We figured that God knew Gabe, that it was God who put the blue-fire yearning in the pit of Gabe's belly in the first place. And it was clear to us that letting our son go so young was the right thing to do for him and his unique needs. We wanted to honor who he was and how his cells were hitched together uniquely. Even so, we knew we were exposing ourselves to pain and potentials unknown, and we would shoulder that burden until he came back to our arms.

The terms and intentions of avant-garde are meant to intersect with all spheres of life, and if we follow that belief to its logical conclusion, then there must be radically pioneering ways of raising children too—ways that cannot be found in manuals or pamphlets.

I wonder if so often we rely on books and other people's parenting styles (which isn't to say those resources don't have their place) because we don't feel we can trust ourselves to make our own wise and distinct decisions and trust the Holy Spirit to help us. The Spirit is the absolute and supreme avant-garde Parent, a Parent who guides outside the rule book and invents new how-tos for those who pause long enough to listen. When all the instructions in the whole world's publications can't advise our specific situations and stories, the Spirit can break through in truly unexpected ways and teach unconventional methods of nurturing and raising our children.

My husband and I have adopted this conviction—that the Spirit-Wind blows uniquely in our lives and helps each individual family operate with its own set of non-status-quo rhythms and functions. Gabe is unlike every other kid on the planet— just as every kid is unlike every other. Holding the value of nonconformity close to our chests, being watchful of our son's uniqueness, and listening closely to the Spirit allowed my husband and me to think outside the boundaries of what is accepted as the norm.

Gabe wasn't technically the age he was supposed to be in order to serve at any of the camps we contacted, but we finally found a place and a people willing to waive their rules to accommodate my son's needs. He was elated. And I was curled up and crying on the bed because I had never imagined during the early kid-raising days—or even the year before—that I would have to let one of my babes go so early.

But maybe I shouldn't have been surprised, considering the way Austin and I had trailed their childhood steps with Richard Rohr and Frederick Buechner and the most haunting, audacious version of Jesus we could possibly tell. Considering our daily morning meditations and prayer practices and church-calendar lessons and character-building conversations and contemplative customs and missional causes. Considering the fervent drum we beat in our home about the upside-down kingdom come and finding out who we are in light of the gospel. Considering that we nudged them from day one to discover their gifts and parse their specific parts and share them freely with the globe.

Yes, Gabe had been born with a nature that said "go," but we had also nurtured him in a way that prepared him early. And

it was shortly after Gabe left us that Austin and I were rock-
ing on the back porch and I turned my head to him, let loose
the tears, and spoke these words: "We've laid a solid foundation
in that boy, and we've surely done more good than harm, and
maybe that's all any parent can hope for. But I have a feeling
this is just the first of so many solo exploratory seasons and trips
before Gabe leaves our nest forever. Dang—this letting-go business totally sucks."

The next morning we received a phone call from Gabe
after ten days of radio silence. (Austin and I had been out of the
country.) We learned that our son had been waking at a manda-
tory five in the morning and working fourteen-hour days doing
everything from mucking stalls to cleaning toilets to mowing
lawns to leading the younger campers in activities and devotions
as a team captain. Clearly this camp and its leaders were extracting the fullness of Gabe's gifts and demanding every bit of energy
he had to give. And Gabe was loving it.

"Mama," he told me, "I am doing so, so good. I cried in the
shower one time because I was homesick, but I feel better and
hey, Mama? I love you so, so, so much, and I am so, so, so, so
grateful you made this happen and let me go. I just can't believe
I'm here, and I'm learning so much and working *so* hard, and I
will never complain again when you ask me to sweep the patio!
I'm praying a lot, and I hear God speaking to me about who I am
and my future. I can't wait to tell you about it!"

For forty-five minutes our son quite literally gushed his
excitement into the phone. And I was a hot-veined, watery mess
the whole time—not just because I missed him, but also because
I finally knew we had made the right decision. Our decision to
send him off extra early might have been unconventional and
questionable to some. But we had listened closely to our lives,
our values, and the shape of our son's soul and allowed the Spirit

to inform and guide us into unpredictable, uncharted territory. We had decided based on who we were, not what we saw other people doing. And Gabe was thriving.

In the meantime, my heavy and sad self was soothed with the high and holy memories Gabe and I had shared—times when the younger boys would sleep and Gabe and I would turn on the soothing music and switch off the lights, hold each other, and sway to the songs. He would tuck his chin on my shoulder, this boy who is my weight and height, and he would clasp my back, and we would sing softly with the tunes while moving our feet gently one way, then the other, and around in small circles.

Hold them close and let them go.

Hold them close and let them go.

Hold them close and they will be ready to go.

And I was reminded while he held me and I held him that when we bring our avant-garde selves to parenting, we're helping our kids become their own avant-garde selves. We are nurturing them to pioneer their own distinct and indigenous path. We're teaching them to rely on the Holy Ghost inside them to guide their choices and surprise them, rather than being informed or defined by prescriptions, formulas, systems, or status quos.

Maybe you're already an avant-garde parent and this story will affirm your own radical ways. Or maybe this is a new idea for you and an avant-garde lens feels like an intriguing way to look at your parental choices. In which case let me say: you have the freedom and, dare I say, the responsibility to craft unique, unorthodox, and (possibly) unheard-of rhythms, experiences, and decisions with and for your family. You do not have to do what everyone else is doing unless it is also what is authentically yours to do.

Do you feel permissioned to examine the inner workings of your home life from this viewpoint? Is there room for you to express and contribute as a family in a unique, avant-garde way? Do you trust yourself to take a risk and get experimental with your family?

Look for the inspiration and permission—make an invitation—to experience God in a singular way. Make the choice to abandon formulas in favor of the unknown, the unbeaten, the unorthodox parenting path.

If you do things a little or a lot wrong, remind yourself that it's okay to win some and lose some—every parent does. If you open your heart to learning, then nothing is wasted ever. And so much can be gained when you go forth with this avant-garde filter for you and yours. These values and actions repeated consistently can provide an enriching experience for everyone—including a world in need of wild and unconventional, Spirit-guided, bandersnatch families.

6

SACRAMENT OF STRANGE

*H*ow are you doing? This is far past the point when I would love to sit with you and talk personally about everything that matters to you and to me. I've shared some stories, and I'd hear yours if we were face-to-face. My favorite thing is when people tell me what they know and I return with what I know and together we dig up old roots with our half-broken and beat-up shovels and simultaneously try to make sense of this beautiful, strange, and sometimes terrible life.

Are you with me? It's just how I believe and do—I don't know how not to go deep. Do you want to keep going deep with me?

I have another story for you supporting the value of crossed-over, avant-garde living, and I hope it means something to you. I hope it sends a nudge to the far reaches of your soul and maybe scrapes just a little bit of free off your bones.

✳

When I was a little girl, my child-eye estimation of my mama was that she was the most uninhibited woman I had ever seen. Sometimes I would peek out a window or through the white spindles at the top of our circular staircase and see her just being her free-spirited self.

When I first started noticing, I didn't really know that her whooping around without constraint and defying convention wasn't typical. It was not unusual to watch her get high from nothing more than a large intake of our clean and countrified air somewhere near the back forty of our farm in Michigan. Then she would let loose with some big unnatural sound and fly through the fields on spinning limbs, and I do swear and declare she opened space with her lungs and legs. Besides the unbridled joy for life exhibited in her spinning limbs and pasture-side yelling, she went to the razor edge of her comfort zone just to touch people that nobody noticed, she made certain to care not at all for keeping up or comparing herself with the Joneses or anyone else, and among other oddities, she created values that opposed culture-wide passions and pursuits. She was less a regular person and more a stranger in a strange land, and in being so she permitted odd kinds of doings and beings. And even to my unseasoned sight it was evident that she wasn't like the other mamas around our parts. "Why isn't she?" I would wonder. Maybe she never did get the status-quo memo.

And yet, despite her abnormalities, all the neighborhood kids wanted to live in our home, wanted to have my mama for their very own nurturer and nestle under the comfort of her slightly strange but love-shadowed wings. She was bright and vibrant and packed with unearthly glory, and I'm sure we took for granted that she was an uncommon creature, that what she was bestowing on us was unprecedented.

Maybe she and we didn't know how much liberty was being

woven through our skin and sinew as a result of her mothering. Maybe she wasn't conscious of what she was doing. Maybe she did it for her own sake, and our soul-sponges just soaked up what seeped down. She was her very own person, and I'm certain she wanted us to exist as our own persons too—not ball-and-chained to civilization's rigid rules of decorum, society's must-dos and must-bes. Drown out the shoulds and the ABCs; let's begin with XYZ—that was her approach to life and to parenting.

Mama made a sacrament out of doing strange things. She arched her neck and blew her weird and wild trumpet and sent society walls tumbling. You could not make her fit in. And that's what prophets do, I think—refuse to fit their squareness into any other geometric shape. Mama never cared what other people thought, and she intentionally misaligned herself with so many ways things were done. She was (and is) a northern-built lighthouse beaming to the darkness where lost ships are longing to set their sails to the home of their own peculiarness.

This isn't to say that she didn't have her own rules and traditions and contraptions she felt enslaved to, but she was constantly asking the questions and taking the actions that would push the boundaries of what was commonly accepted behavior and belief—even if it took her ten years to undo something that systemized her insides. My mama was as free as she could be within the context she understood, and it was more than enough to leave an indelible impression on me.

I lost my way for a little while, for more than a decade or so. As a teenager I remember wishing that my mama could be more like other moms because she embarrassed me sometimes with her unbridled spirit. Maybe Mama didn't want to fit in, but I did. I wanted so badly to be "normal" and liked and accepted—wanted those things far more than I wanted to be my very own precious self.

But there came a time when the great and gracious Spirit said enough is enough and providentially appointed people to help me find my way back to the truth of my parts and particulars. One of those appointed people was (and is) our Anglican priest friend, Johnny.

Johnny blew into our lives gusty-storm style, swelling through our doorway bigger than a rush of rain at hurricane speed. I conceptualize him quite frequently in my imagination, and he is always wearing this big and billowing prophet's robe with ancient frays and patterns. Dust swirls around his purposefully treading feet, kicked alive in the wake of the good disaster he brings. For Johnny's kind of disaster, I have found, is right for the soul.

With his billowing robes and the Wind behind his back and clear aim in his eyes, Johnny thundered through one day and squalled against our soul spaces to tell us, "Your boats are full of holes!" Then he proceeded to walk alongside us, inch by devastating inch, as we learned how to build solid vessels while still being tossed and torn about in the middle of life's high seas.

The holes that Johnny spoke of were actually the fortresses of our false selves. We were living defensively behind molds, conformity, status quo, religious spirits, herd mentalities, and so forth. We were poster children for not-avant-garde. And Johnny, with his gift for damaging molds into dust and splitting religious spirits seven hundred ways before Sunday morning, was an instrument of our necessary undoing. The questions he asked, the conversations he initiated, the times he got an inch from our faces and inspired us to rethink and reexamine our lives and beliefs and values—all the methods he used—truly made our

stout hearts nearly faint and rigid bums squirm in our standardized seats. He was a prophet with his own strange trumpet. He
never strode the streets actually shouting and buck naked, but he
might as well have done that, so free was he.

When this strangeness of Johnny's crashed into me thirteen
years ago, something long dormant ruptured loose, then, wide
inside my rib-bone region. It prompted me to scurry down to
the bowels of my being and begin resuscitating my roots. And
what came from this process was my own really wild me. My
self-protective, conforming walls of brick and mortar crumbled
left, right, and center from the audacious and prodigious permission I received from my friend.

Johnny's artfully expressed eccentricities made me feel like I
could come out with all my closet oddities and dare to be dangerous. And *dangerous* is the exact right word if we're talking about
what a threat it is to the entire watching world when someone
comes undone to be born again more alive than ever before.

When I met Johnny, I was reminded of my mom and how she
would demolish the walls around us just by being true to herself
and not caring if she was acting the way people were supposed
to or that she might look stupid in front of anyone's face. She
and Johnny and people like them blast themselves against the
stones the world has erected, beat them down with all the passion
of undressed prophets, and make a sacrament out of being off-
center. They are a little mad, a whole lot foolish and fearless, but
they no doubt breathe forward the right messages for my time,
your time—our time.

Because we suffer from an epidemic of sameness in this society and in our faith traditions, we desperately need to create a

sacrament out of strangeness, make a value of it, and write it on our foreheads and the bathroom mirror or the doorframe next to the pencil lead marking our kids' last birthday heights. Why would you defile your thisness with everyone else's thatness?

In so many corners of our culture it is strange to be yourself. So be strange, okay? You're not alone. We need to remember how to be crazy just for crazy's sake, how not to be normal, how to lose some of our appropriateness and let the Spirit take over. The Spirit is way more wild than we are, and only after abandoning ourselves totally can we blow the weird, primitive, and fearless trumpets the Father provided when he created us.

Maybe you're wondering why it's important to embrace your strangeness. Or maybe you can't imagine mustering enough energy to care your way out of the systems and schemes and structures, out of the organizations and knots and walls and codes that corner and order you. If that's true, let me ask you some questions:

Do you have a reverence for the holy ash you are?

Do you not know, have you not heard that your dimensions and textures and humors will never happen again on the earth, ever?

It's time to fall back into the Potter's hand and discover you can be born again, again. He'll touch you back into your own shape, return you to your own strangeness as many times as it takes for you to be you. Even if you have to ask a thousand times before your next birthday, he is patient in saving the size and specialness of your true self because he knows the great chorus is meant to include the song that you alone can sing; he knows it is an injustice to the global tribe if your notes aren't true to your design.

*

Since we are talking about making a sacrament out of being a little or a lot strange, then you might be interested that St. Augustine defines *sacrament* as "an outward and visible sign of an inward and invisible grace." Let's be a people who have the inward grace to have an outward weirdness. And when I say *weirdness*, I don't mean that everyone should paint geometric rainbows on their faces or dance around their cul-de-sacs wearing feathered headdresses. And I don't mean that you should be hollering and horsing around when your own natural weirdness tends toward quiet and calm. Your outward weirdness is just the audacity to be you, different from me and Bob and your great-aunt Betty or her neighbor's son Bill. Don't be afraid to be a fool—or to seem a fool. You are held by a wideness so huge you can never step outside of it.

And now that I'm a mama, I am aiming true and fueling hard the fire inside me to burn just a little to the far left or distant right of normal so I can deposit in our kids the same seed my mama sowed in me—an avant-garde approach to identity and life. Sometimes I will very intentionally take a moment out of any ordinary piece of time and purpose myself to lose all appropriateness, letting Spirit take over my body. Just for practice, you know, so that I don't get too comfortable or tempted to slip into everyone's orthodox. And sometimes the Peculiar just happens to me and I surrender to it, and I'm not surprised to find my feet let loose and my arms stretched wide like flesh-wings, my whole body serpentining through a public parking lot, hollering with aliveness in front of the immediate gaping viewers.

When I go all weird like that, maybe because the breeze has just the perfect degree of balm to it and slides elegantly across my bared skin, my younger two boys go all goofy with excitement, and my oldest smiles all the way to his lit-up eyes. "Mama," he says with a small shake of his adolescent head, "you're the craziest person I know."

With tears of joy I bare-teeth beam back at him and tell him he could pay me no deeper compliment. And I know he thinks the same crazy-mama thought when I bellow my prayers in the car while driving through the city streets or I dance underwear-style in my bathroom to my favorite songs or sing so strong my voice comes out hoarse. I am the queen of nonsequiturs and skipping down the sidewalks in the rain for all the neighbors to see. I can't control spontaneous spots of awkwardness. And yet I'm only half as weird as I long to be.

I'm getting there, though. The closer I get to the divine gaze, the more liberated I become. And whenever I am as close to being me as I possibly can be, when I'm living like I'm naked inside, I feel dark things breaking down and chains crashing undone in the atmosphere inside and also all around my body. Even better is when the son who has the most inhibitions starts hollering his prayers through the house or with his head hanging out the vehicle window. The recognition that history is repeating itself intoxicates me. I hope to God these boys will forever know the fruit of letting a little wild take over, even when they're grown and the rules are miles wide and anchors deep.

I pray that they will make a sacrament out of being a little strange. Because these world-walls sometimes feel thicker than ancient Jericho's, but when we all blow our own fearless, avant-garde trumpets, the stones come crashing down around our cities, and we the people seem to break a little open and undone.

Again, I'm not advocating for everyone to be a blustery prophet like Johnny. If that happened, the whole globe would certainly suck itself into a vortex. Johnny himself wouldn't want that. He's the anti-formula guy. Making others in his image has never been his thing.

Johnny never offered me a blueprint to follow when he came into my life. But his sacramental strangeness was an invitation and permission for me to become myself. And now I am wondering if you might need someone to blow into your comfortable or conformed spaces and speak a "giddyup" or a "let's go."

Why? Because the Maker covets the way he knit you together stranger than anyone else. Which is to say: he made you different on purpose. Mimicking the methods and movements of other people is one big smasher of your rare intellect and animation and an affront to the on-purpose of your design.

Take a minute in the quiet and scan your invisible insides. What percentage of you is original like you were born to be, and what percentage of you is owned by society's systems and institutions and formulas for fun and happiness and rules for right living that don't allow for the sacrament of your own strangeness?

If you don't like the percentages, if you're neck deep in a pile of human-made systems, then change the game or change the channel or change the music or turn the blasted, befuddled tables. If you can't find the sacrament of your strangeness or the courage to go headlong after it, you might have made your very own flesh temple—your very own house of worship—into something it wasn't built to be. And it's time to change that.

"How?" you may say. "How do I realize the essence of my true identity? How do I dismantle and bump and knock things around enough inside me that they begin to break loose and I get free?"

Here's a universal directive: ask.

Lie down on your own flat back in a dark and quiet space and beseech the Almighty as if your whole self is burning from that one question: "What systems do I subscribe to that are actually killing me, and how do I begin upending and breaking away from those systems?" Listen hard, and prepare for a pilgrimage.

But don't go it alone. Find a friend or a whole community to take this journey with you. Remind yourself that the Spirit is also there to walk with you—that's what the Spirit does.

And then . . . begin.

Peel back your distractions and consumptions, your mind wars and whatnot. Listen for as long as it takes to discern one thing, one response, one system, and start there. Inch by inch or brick by brick, tear it apart and throw it down and burst forth from the destruction of it with the light of a thousand rising suns. I'm certain that's what your true self looks like—like your skin is on holy fire and your eyes are lit like beacons from within.

And don't stop there. Keep on going. The goal is to recover, reimagine, restore, reorganize, redeem, renew, resurrect . . . your own self in Christ. The goal is to cross over all your definitions.

Refuse to indulge society's systems and expectations any longer. Choose instead to devote yourself to a contemplative, avant-garde union with the divine. And you will naturally, spontaneously spread out and awake into wonderful and bizarre wholeness.

And now for a little interlude.

We've wrapped up the theme of avant-garde, and by now I'm hoping you feel a spacious invitation to embrace a new or expanded life lens. I'm also hoping you feel bold enough to reclaim the birthright of your peculiar uniqueness, a uniqueness that is hardly supported by the fanciful and flaky culture we live in. Our culture commands us to find our identities in the rapidly shifting moods and ideas informed by the manipulations and schemes of society.

Replace that falsehood with this fact: your true, avant-garde identity comes from within. It is native to who you are, the most fundamental thing about you. Reach through and touch it; choose it to be the filter that sits behind your eyeballs informing the way in which you approach and view the world. Do you want it?

Do you want it?

Let your answer be a "yes," I pray. I pray from my heart pressed to the ground and with every five-and-a-half-feet of me that you sense enough liberty to arrive at your daily, nitty-gritty, mundane existence with the intention of a nonconformist, with radical and unorthodox permission to grasp the media in front of you with a bent against the world's systems and the status quo. Are you with me?

Are you with me?

If you're with me and you have the purpose and pang of a vanguardist in your tissue, between your lungs and bones, would you harness what you know of yourself and all your extra energetic atoms and come close to me as I invite you to examine three more themes? I want to tell you stories of more and wide and high, and I want us to run to the four corners of this round earth looking for what's beautiful and true.

Let's go together because this next special little something we're investigating is the stuff of whispers and intimacy, bonfires and shared love. It's the stuff of us if we were neighbors and our desires walked in the space of similar.

Alchemy

7

REDEFINING ALCHEMY

For thirty-four years now I've been waltzing and crashing and burning around the sun, and with every dip and arch and turn and misstep and face plant, I'm unfurling into more of who I was born to be—discovering dots, connecting threads, sketching ideas, and chasing the Spirit around all the places I can think of just so I can ask her all the questions that come bursting from the bowels of my being.

More than five years ago I asked so many certain questions and listened long enough to learn a new reality about myself. You might find this reality strange, or you might consider it entirely refreshing. But here it is either which way: I am, by inherent design, an alchemist (and you are too, but I'll get to that later).

I am an alchemist.

What I believe it means to be an alchemist in the twenty-first century is the same as what it meant to be an alchemist in the first century, but not the same as what most people think it means. (Did I just confuse you? Because I think I just confused myself!)

No, I cannot turn scrap metal into storehouses of gleaming gold the way medieval philosophers tried so hard to do. (They couldn't do it either.) But there's a subdefinition for *alchemy* that applies not only to the Jesus-filled gospel accounts, but also to our everyday lives. According to dictionary.com, *alchemy* is "any magical power or process of transmuting a common substance, usually of little value, into a substance of great value."

Let's pause here for a second because I'm wondering if you might have a hang-up with the *magical* word? How do you define magic? What do you think of when you hear it? Dark arts? Wizardry? Witchcraft? Voodoo?

Not me. Not necessarily.

I think of Jesus and all the miracles he performed with nothing more than ordinary, everyday, readily available supplies—mud, spit, loaves, flesh, fishes . . . and Spirit. That is my foundational reference point when I use the word *magic*.

I'm not Jesus, obviously, and I don't do miracles the way they are usually understood. So maybe it's a stretch to announce that I am an alchemist. But bear with me, and I'll show you more of what I mean.

I woke up early on a Wednesday, and the sky was still dark, strung with a slice of crescent moon and millions of far-out star-specks. The blackness outside was full of cooing—soothing, soundless songs—and the house was strangely quiet with our three resident noisemakers recharging in their beds. I sat myself in the spot where the Spirit and I have our predawn meetings. And there in that special space, with the low light and hushed tones of home, I felt compelled from deep beneath my epidermis to get my fingers out and begin rolling the air between the tips of them just so I could touch what nothing-molecules felt like.

And just like that, a common moment of seemingly little value was transmuted into a substantial moment of great value.

As I sat there with my eyes sealed and my mouth moving lightly with the "meet with me" words and the pads of my fingers gently wrapping and rolling around the air, I sensed the peeling back of the atmosphere and the presence of one very singular Spirit reveal herself and awaken my faculties even further—taste, touch, hear, see, and smell all pulled apart yet intertwined, spread out and willing to enter the land beyond clocks and calendars while also being embedded in the land of here and now.

My senses and the air came together in luminous love, and greater awareness was born in a room composed of nothing more than furniture and floorboards and flesh. Spirit revealed herself, and she and I communed in this great fusing of my ordinary with heaven's extraordinary, mixing in the silence for what felt like a speck of real time—heaven and earth, dust and divine.

To me, that's real-life alchemy. The kingdom of heaven is always less than a speck or a step away, and if we take a fragment of any day and slow our souls to see it, we are actually choosing to become alchemists, refining and redefining every single mundane moment.

By inviting the great Alchemist to mix with us—unite with us—we embody the Presence that purposes an ordinary act into meaning more than meets the common eye. This happens on earth as it is in heaven. And it doesn't necessarily mean that the hustle and bustle and urgency of the hour and the list you have in your hand gets turned off or set aside. But somehow an awareness burgeons and the intention changes and humble elements like morning time and dark air, the oatmeal on the stove and the tattoo of your heart, are transformed into something eternal and precious.

Magic indeed. But this is no cheap trick, no charlatan conjuring. This is what happens when we choose to be a vessel for priceless pieces of heaven right here on the carnal terrain where our feet are bound.

All it took for the Creator of the cosmos to make something more of my earthly elements on that particular Wednesday was just a tiny moment and a bit of space and all my intention. All it took was a belief that at any occasion the curtain to the physical world could be pulled back to reveal the mystical, the mysterious, the magical.

I decided that very day that I was born to be an alchemist.

I decided to become an air roller because I am every which way determined not to miss a single microscopic, ordinary thing.

I don't have to wonder very long to know who the original Alchemist was and is and is to come, and you must know I'm thinking of that long-ago dust-spread being blown full with Holy Ghost breath, and up from the bits of dirt came the shape of sinew and spine and socket, humanity birthed from the life force of the living God. His breath became ours, and intimacy was born on the earth. One enchanted exhalation from the lungs of the great Alchemist, and what was practically nothing was made to be the most valuable something, with souls and dreams and a capacity to create. We are sons and daughters burst forth from ashes, rising flesh to carry on the commissioned work of the Alchemist.

Glory is already down everywhere, waiting to be invited into our nothing. We cannot escape the encompassing presence of God because it fills the final bit of everything right down to the last atom in a shaft of sunlight receding below the edge of the globe. Can heaven invade and increase any further or go any lower on her knees to get our notice? She presses into all our spaces and senses, begging for us to make something important and beautiful and lasting with her. Unless we slow long enough and undress ourselves and our lives, sit in the dirt under a blanket of silence, we'll never have the awareness and ability to engage the Presence's attention.

Being an alchemist is nothing if not presenting oneself as a deep adorer of the divine, communing for the purpose of transforming the unnoticeable by the very act of noticing. The transmuting magic of value and love is infused into the most common of substances until they become, to the beholder, a substance of priceless worth. The most readily available common substance is our very own typical time, our daily drudgery. But when we choose to roll the air, these humdrum moments become rich and filled full with amazement.

My friend Johnny pens it like this in his personal manifesto: "For every breath of this beating life, I have searched for another way to find paradise lost; a place I once called home—not in the higher residence of eternity but in the soil of earth's heaven, a common land." And I am speaking the same concept in this language of alchemy. Paradise is lost but can be found again and again and again by me and you and right now in the common land of earth's heaven, in the base materials at the tips of eighty billion fingers.

I'm led by alchemy to remember every redemption story I've ever heard and all the tales of burned-down ashes turning toward raised-up beauty because the original Alchemist breathes the magic-wielding breath of value and love. And we, this eclectic blend of alchemist apprentices who follow the Master—it is our commission to each carry forward in our own weird ways this wild-hearted championing of the impossible. We are the pupils and perpetrators of wonder, and for the sake of all that is sacred we must never give up transmuting, never ever falter from touching the air with the flesh of our hands and imagining this unassuming element we take for granted is worth so much more than we often remember.

Alchemy—it's as near and necessary as our next breath and next breath and next breath. We breathe Spirit in while she sustains us, slowing all our molecules to become miracles. Today and tomorrow and until the hereafter we've already been given eyes to see and ears to hear and hearts to understand and throats to drink down and deep of the divine, every miraculous ounce that we can swallow.

It's your decision how you use the sacred gifts that are already yours. But know this: ordinary days are the very stage on which alchemy desires to appear. You can sink into the celestial right in the midst of everything else—with that baby at your chapped breast and the mud tracks on the carpet and the stranger on the corner holding out a McDonald's cup for coins.

This kind of communion is what we have been built for—to make love with the Spirit every possible moment. Don't let her go, and she will not stop haunting you. Every morning aim to be as porous as a person can be while stretching every bit of your body toward the risen Son.

Open and wide is the best way to sponge up the whole life experience. And when we sponge up whatever atoms our openness and wideness allow, it's then that we uncover one or two more mysteries at a time, soaked-up truths to cherish softly and scribble on the scratchpad of our souls, the place where whispers and secrets get harbored safe within us for eternity at least.

Try this at home. (This is me being directive.) Slow down; open your eyes and your heart as wide as they can go. And watch for the miraculous in the unfolding heart of the everyday.

Alchemy, as I've already hinted, has its historical and foundational roots in the Middle Ages. During that era, alchemy was an experimental scientific process that aimed to achieve the transmutation of base metals into gold, which was considered crazy. But the purpose wasn't just shiny decoration. To these questing medieval chemists, gold represented the universal panacea, even a way to indefinitely prolong life. I have wondered if those medieval scientists looked at the glories and delicacies of the natural world around them and imagined that magic had to be possible and therefore believed that somehow and someway they could harness its properties.

But I think those first alchemists approached alchemy all wrong, and here's the most important redefining part of this chapter—the crossing over of alchemy. Historically alchemists have wanted alchemy to work for their own sakes. They aimed for magic with wealth, health, and power in mind. But kingdom alchemy only works for Christ's sake. It happens when we use the stuff of heaven to reveal the inherent value of the basest and lowliest.

Which brings us back to the subdefinition I spoke of earlier: "Alchemy is any magical power or process of transmuting a common substance, usually of little value, into a substance of great value." Which, I think, is much closer to a kingdom definition of alchemy, especially if you are contemplating the life of Jesus and all his stories of making something out of nothing:

Alchemy is what sits between water and wine.

Alchemy is what waits between five loaves, two fish, and five thousand ravenous people.

Alchemy rests in the space between a blind man and his sight.

Alchemy is what made death on the cross an act of salvation for billions of people.

There's more.

Alchemy is also George Washington Carver examining a lowly peanut and dreaming up three hundred uses for it.

Alchemy is when Picasso, one of the most influential artists of the twentieth century, cofounded several new creative movements, including collage, constructed sculpture, and Cubism.

It's a Chicago nanny taking transcendent pictures of strangers on a Chicago street or a mom making a meal from the lowly bits and pieces of an almost empty fridge.

Most important of all, alchemy is simply sitting in one space long enough to watch the sun go down and feeling reborn from it.

It's washing your baby in the bath and witnessing the manifest glory of God on the surface of that slippery skin.

It's walking down a city street and seeing the Spirit surrounding and invading the whole of everything and everyone.

It's catching the sunlight through the trees in such a way that a moment becomes a portal to the divine.

Alchemy, in other words, is the process of seeing and releasing the stuff of heaven that waits in the air around you. You become an alchemist when you discern and receive what's already and everywhere available.

Alchemy on the other side of Jesus is the accessing of the celestial for the sake of building and bringing the kingdom right now.

When Jesus used his brand of alchemy, he did it for the sake of exposing the kingdom. He often took a common substance with no recognized value—like dirt and spit—and used it to heal the suffering and to reveal something greater of the Father. Kingdom alchemy believes that you can take a substance of little worth and unveil it as treasure—not for the purpose of building towers or making names for ourselves or turning metal into gold, but to bring heaven to earth right now, the way Jesus did.

Medieval alchemists found neither the universal panacea nor the ability to make metal into gold because they were looking in all the wrong places with all the wrong intentions. They wanted the magic for themselves; they wanted to gain. But kingdom alchemists are not here to gain; they're here to give.

The kingdom alchemist knows that heaven wants to be found, that God's glory is sitting everywhere, hidden in plain sight. The kingdom alchemist partners with the Spirit to make water into wine or to transform any mundane moment into an eternal imprint. And it's all for a single purpose: to make God seen and known so we can experience a lover's intimacy with the divine. This *is* the universal panacea, the only elixir that yields eternal life. It's the only magic that will turn a lead-filled world to gold.

Do you believe that being an alchemist is within you?

Do you believe that you were made to walk your avant-garde molecules toward the ordinary, everyday stuff around you and radically, oddly, uniquely transform it into something miraculous?

Do you want to take the seemingly insignificant pieces and particles of life and stare at them and stretch them apart and taste them under a microscope and hear the vibrations on your tongue and smell them in the ways that only you can, until their value and the depth of their crossed-over definition is revealed before your eyes and right in front of the watching world?

Let's sit in the present together with our bowl or backpack or basket full of nothing until those substances labeled "little value" become the substances of greatest value, until the worth of the kingdom inside them is finally, fully realized.

8

YOU ARE AN ALCHEMIST

We live in an utterly enchanted universe, but how often do we perceive and engage with the magical nature of our world?

We long for the evidence that there is more to life than what we can see and touch and feel, but how often do we pause in our physical, practical paces and let ourselves be spellbound by the living Spirit?

We've been given access to a foretaste of heaven, but how often do we allow the supernatural realm to pierce through our earthly lives?

I just asked the same question three ways because most of us really need to investigate what patterns and systems and beliefs keep us from being present, keep us from being wonder-workers revealing the true kingdom, keep us from being tender, careful alchemists by which the higher miracles and mysteries are especially revealed.

And in response to that belief, I have spent countless hours cultivating in our three sons the methods and intentions of a kingdom alchemist, hoping they will learn how to participate in exposing and enjoying all things ordinary for their actual and acute extraordinary value.

This cultivation process takes on many forms, but I'm going to give you one example of what it looks like on an average morning in our home so that you can begin imagining for yourself ways of nurturing the alchemist in you and yours.

We're touching one another knee-to-knee in a circle on the floor, and I invite my three sons to enter the next twenty minutes with a fully invested heart, ready for the divine to be revealed in our midst. Their faces are fervent when I lean over and whisper soft and sure, saying words akin to this:

> Come closer, my dear sons, because I have something to show you of life and God and the fabric of the universe. This is a tool for your toolboxes—open them, and I'll drop it in. I want your gravity-bound beings to fly, and this is how you connect with truth and get yourselves as free as bald eagles soaring into the whipping wind.
>
> Shut your eyes and calm your limbs and lungs; slow down to breathe deep from your belly-place. We have a meeting with the stuff of heaven right here in this room. There is nothing more important than this now-space. Imagine holding time in your very palms and tell the relentless ticking to still. We've got communion to do—breathe deep again and again, and every time you exhale, let go of your negative feelings and distractions and agitations. Cleanse your palates and inhale the clean air. The Spirit is in the wings of each molecule and moment. Visualize your hearts and heads and hands opening and posture yourselves to receive.
>
> Now that your receptors are expanded, imagine the living God is reaching exactly for your two hands. Imagine

he is leading you somewhere special today just to speak words over your clean and uncluttered bodies. Picture these Almighty words descending from the sky, drifting down like petals from heaven—soft, colorful flakes of letters landing on your hair and skin and crisscrossed legs. Imagine your mind broadening to accept these word-gifts from God. Scoop them to your soul and tell me what he's saying to you today.

Be still; be silent.

Listen. Can you hear them? Receive!

This is the language and method of a mystic-hearted mama teaching her children how to be available and au naturel before the living Christ, contemplative and spread wide in their spirits, able to accept and participate in the alchemy of turning everyday moments of meditation and mindfulness into heaven on earth right now.

Let's pause here for a second because I'm wondering again if reading words like *mystic* and *meditation* and *mindfulness* strikes an uncomfortable chord. In some Christian circles these words and practices are not only taboo but also referenced as satanic. And yet there's a long history of Christian mysticism, believers seeking deeper union with Christ through meditative practices.

Listen to my heartbeat: when I spend time in meditation (or when I encourage our boys to do so), I am merely attempting to focus my undivided attention on the love of God embodied in the person of Jesus, dwelling on the attributes of the One my whole being yearns for. This ongoing participation with the Presence centers my soul and allows for my disorder and imperfection to be held perfectly in divine union. To me, this holy joining is true spirituality—so simple, so beautiful, so right— and I pass this down with the desire that our children, too, carry forward the art of mysticism, an ongoing routine of inner experience or "oneness" with God, to their children.

I'm reminded here of Shakespeare and his famous words from *Romeo and Juliet*:

> *What's in a name? that which we call a rose*
> *By any other name would smell as sweet.*[1]

The names of things do not necessarily affect what they really are. Meditation and the resulting mysticism can resemble the practice of what some faith traditions commonly refer to as "quiet time." Even so, *meditation* aligns and defines more accurately the way in which I engage with the Spirit, and *mysticism* aligns and defines more accurately with the desired and actual outcome of that engagement.

By keeping our hearts and mind spaces open long enough for our spirits to sense the invisible material, by choosing to be vulnerable before a moment, we'll know that the Spirit is always waiting for us—the receiving stations—to wake up to her undeniable, incessant Presence. And once you've cleared your receptors and I've cleared mine, we become alchemists actively engaging in heaven.

Catherine of Siena (a famous Christian mystic) is quoted as saying, "All the way to heaven is heaven because [Jesus] said, 'I am the way.'"[2]

By following the ways of Jesus, you and I and everyone else have already been gifted with the tools to experience heaven all the way to heaven. Sometimes the opportunity comes to us effortlessly, and sometimes we can help it happen by choosing a room, an attitude, a specific hour or ten minutes or two seconds of the day; by changing the lighting, the pace of our breath, the depth of our perception; by expanding our skin and sinking into the bottom floor of our souls to co-make something rare and exquisite with the Alchemist.

There are occasions when the urge for alchemy nudges me awake and I crawl from my covers at night when the whole house is sleeping. I sit in my striped chair in the living room—without the light, without my phone, without any distraction whatsoever—and I open up to the Holy Spirit: "You have come to me, and I have come to you." And just as soon as it's said, I am all messed up from the inside, speechless at the brilliance of being together. And sitting with darkness and silence and the tears I don't understand—being with my Love—leaves me with an ache of want so big I sense I could expire from it. No one but us is a witness to the watering and wanting, to the fiery clamp of my palms on both armrests, the veins growing hot in my neck. This is a personal practice of noticing that I've adopted from what I've seen Jesus do when he would go alone to the mountain to pray—taking time that looks like nothing on the outside and turning it into gold.

Do you already practice alchemy by another name—quiet time, meditation, prayer moments, setting aside space and place to connect with the divine? If not, it's so clean and uncomplicated and worth the practice. Where are you right now? What room are you in? Who's with you, or are you alone? I'm writing this to you from an unassuming spot in my bedroom, and everything on the surface seems ordinary until I choose to make a small stop and recognize the Otherness inside and around me. And that recognition is like being wrapped in an eternal experience—heaven on earth.

Heaven, you see, isn't just about the future. Heaven is right now in my heart, in my humdrum, in my home, and I am transported there by having eyes that see and ears that hear and a heart that understands the mysteries of the menial.

The alchemist knows that heaven is a part of a summer evening campfire and marshmallows on sticks carved with pocketknives and yoga on the dock at sundown and the iridescent suds of your dirty dishwater. Heaven is on your kitchen countertop. It's an unseen guest at the dining room dinner table. It's knit within your early morning get-out-the-door routine. Heaven is in your heartbeat and your next breath and the tap of your digits against the typing keys. Heaven is everything between the earth and the edge of the visible world and beyond Vega and down to the depths of the deepest black hole.

Heaven is anywhere we choose to allow the Spirit of God to transmute our ephemeral into eternal, our waters into wine, our mustard seeds into movable mountains, our stale pieces of bread into the very body of Christ.

Jesus said, "The person who trusts me will not only do what I'm doing but even greater things" (John 14:12). But how often do these "greater things" remain undone because we keep ourselves cut off from the Source that would allow the alchemist in all of us to come alive?

Here is your opportunity: put on your avant-garde glasses and walk straight into the stuff of heaven and transmute a moment into something you've never previously imagined.

Notice.

Practice.

Intend.

Kneel before heaven, receive, and say *yes!*

And then . . . follow.

Our bodies were made for—and only for—two words in all the known galaxies, and those two words are simply, profoundly, hauntingly, "Follow me." Those two words are the underpinning to every other exquisite and legitimate and noble thing.

The first time I truly heard Jesus say, "Follow me," I decided to do so earnestly, as much as I am able. I attempt to do what I see him doing and go where I see him going. And throughout the Gospels I see the continual incantation and communion of "on earth as it is in heaven."

I see Jesus as a walking atmosphere of transmutation, a living atmosphere of lead into gold. Let's follow him into the mud and spit and grit of the world and do something magical with it—turn it around, upside down, backward if necessary. Believe that the fairy tale is real.

After preparing and posturing our boys, guiding their bodies, minds, and spirits to harmonize with the symphonies and melodies of the Maker, I commission each to his own quiet corner to record the messages God impresses upon his chest. I teach them to bring just who they uniquely are to their meetings so they will come away with an encounter that is original to them.

This is my version of letting the little children come to him, cultivating holy territory for the young ones to learn the disciplines of connecting with the naked presence of God without restraint or barriers. I teach them how to touch the Air, breath the Air, taste the Air, become one with the Air. Because this alchemy—this engagement with the stuff of heaven—is romance 101. It's my way of matchmaking the greatest love affair of their lives, a love affair I hope will lead them to becoming Holy Spirit revolutionaries, opening portals to the supernatural across the land and sea and sky, living the truth of kingdom come.

From our living room meditation we go out into the world,

and I help them imagine what an invitation to alchemy looks like at the farmer's market or on a mindful hike through deep creation or while eating dinner at Shake Shack before a concert on the green, or while traveling to Vermont or Connecticut or Michigan or overseas.

The whole wide world is our cathedral, a meeting place for communing with God, and by teaching this I welcome our boys to their own priesthood. "Gabe, Seth, and Jude—sons of Adam, knit of God—practice alchemy on the altar of your ordinary lives, and the intimacy that is intrinsic in you and accessible any-time, anywhere, without walls or programs or formulas to hold you back, will give birth to the stuff of miracles."

Each place we go provides an opportunity for me to invite them to engage with divinity differently. Each visit or encounter, each piece of landscape or set of circumstances, prompts the ques-tion, "How can alchemy happen here?" What is Spirit waiting for me to do? Wash the laundry or the dishes or your own skin; go to the soup kitchen or the corner store or California and open your soul, stretch your senses, roll the air. Make love with heaven on every little bit of earth because this is how kingdom incarnates. This is how Jesus comes now, while we wait for "soon."

I illustrate to our boys this essential axiom so they will know what's absolutely real, so they know that the physical world is a temporary, beautiful gateway to the everlasting, so they know how to prostrate themselves before the face of God and learn to trace the divine features—cracks, crevices, wrinkles, eyelashes, lips, cheekbones, pores, smile lines—with the tips of awestruck fingers and come away with palms out, lifted, and offered as a show-and-tell of the glittering, inconceivable Truth.

I am raising little alchemists, inviting their bodies, minds, and spirits to practice heaven right now—nurturing them to be perceptive human beings who give credence to the lowly and unrecognizable. No matter where they find themselves or who they continue to become, I hope this deep, foundational, spiritual connection will be the original and real lifeblood of their existence.

Do you believe that within you are the components it takes to be an alchemist?

What would it look like for you to take the uniqueness of your true, avant-garde self and open up to the stuff of heaven?

Just as I endeavor to lead my sons in the way of alchemy, I'm inviting you to try your hand at transmutation. Alchemy sits in the air like a pregnant woman, and I am the midwife giving birth to conversion, inviting the Presence to metamorphose our moments.

Don't look away; don't turn to the right or the left. Curve your limbs into the lap of Holiness and tuck yourself in for an intimate sit. Let yourself be haunted by the heavenly. Wait for it. Drink. Taste and see.

It is not a passive enterprise to fall into the abyss of this foundational truth. Set aside occasions to prepare the soil of your heart for planting Spirit seeds, and divine presence will be a gift you unwrap in real time.

Don't waste time on things that are detached from the original intention of oneness with the Holy Spirit. Rather, try to creatively manifest in your every day the vibrations of the living God, a God who is as accessible and available as every breath you let in and out. Attend to the very thing you do constantly, and believe in the surprise of the Spirit.

Believe that anything at any time is possible.

9

THE ALCHEMIC POTENTIAL
OF DIRTY FEET

It had been a whole long-haul season of the back-breaking, sweat-making, happy-faking kind of struggle. Here I was nearing the end of another homeschool study year, and for some irritating reason I felt like I was naked-knee crawling and dry-throat panting to a desert finish line that seemed to be a mirage somewhere in the middle of the godforsaken Sahara.

I'm what psychologist Elaine Aron calls a Highly Sensitive Person (HSP).[1] I'm also an introvert who spends all day, every day, with people. And even though these people are my people, the emotional energy output required is Everest-sized. Plus these young people of mine happen to be boys, and I am a girl. And while none of us fit neatly into the sweeping gender generalizations, we are most certainly *not* the same.

More to the point, there are a couple of areas where my boys and I are total opposites. For example, I love the volume level referred to as "quiet," while each thing they do and are and say is LOUD!!!!!!! I love to move slowly and gently, while they race from every which thing, every which way, all the time, like there's a blazing blue fire lit right behind their tiny hineys.

So on this particular day I arrived at the pulled-thinnest place I'd been in a long while. And when an early morning altercation broke out between the boys, I started sobbing before I could even speak. At the same sobbing time, my trembling hands happened to be holding an aluminum container full of multi-colored markers and other art materials, and let me go ahead and tell you I held the corners of that container in a death grip just so I wouldn't give it rage-persuaded flying lessons across the living room or into the next county. I removed myself from the scene of near crime by walking my weary, slumped-over shoulders and hurting heart out the door and down the sidewalk so I could breathe deep before I hurt someone—and by "someone" I don't mean myself.

We've all been there, right? The days or weeks or whole multiple months that bust your heart apart and make you bawl baby-like and go berserk as if there were bats in your belfry.

As far as I've heard, every parent slams face-first into how ridiculously hard ordinary life can be with its herd of hoodlums and hoydens and its routine drudgery and all the running around and to-do lists and laundry and late nights. And how do we possibly apply the high shimmery stuff of kingdom alchemy to our maddening everyday world of sibling squabbles and unwashed dishes and floors and homework help?

How do we transform the ordinariness of our very ordinary lives?

There are more than a thousand ways to kneel and kiss the skin of the Spirit, to fold open and bathe in the gaze of God, to give the stuff of heaven exclusive opportunity to slip in softly and speak the light-filled words that would remodel our situations, our thinkings, our moments, and our energy. And sometimes when I'm about to throw the markers and scream at the living room walls and do injury to the children, when I'm too peeved or distracted or noisy for Spirit to reach me, she'll come to my conscience in the middle of the night because she can get to me quick and pointed when I'm calm and surrounded by darkness, when my mind is still and silent.

She comes to me when my ears are clear, when I'm fragile and on the brink of breaking apart, giving up, or going crazy. And she invites me to another vantage point, a new view where I can reimagine the ordinariness of my life, especially as it relates to parenting. She tells me by way of her own old words how to bring the magical stuff of heaven into the hubbub and busyness and boy-raising. Her own old words, which were also Jesus' words when he said them to his frazzled friend Martha, who was annoyed at her sister Mary for not helping serve dinner:

> The Master said, "Martha, dear Martha, you're fussing far too much and getting yourself worked up over nothing. One thing only is essential, and Mary has chosen it—it's the main course, and won't be taken from her." (Luke 10:42)

"One thing only is essential . . . it's the main course," he says.

And the one essential main course he was speaking of was himself, and the way Mary sat before him and hung on every word he said was the right choice. On a later occasion, while Martha was busy serving again, Mary knelt to bathe his feet with fragrant oil and wiped them with her hair, serving him in her own unique way (John 12:1–3). But for now, Mary was simply sitting, and Martha was peeved.

Martha, dear Martha, was so caught up in the size and stack of her own ordinary agenda, she forgot that the way to experience heaven on her humdrum earth was to fall flat before the feet of Jesus and glue herself to his every extraordinary, life-giving syllable. She was so distracted serving and fixing and being hospitable, doing all the right and good things, that she lost track of what mattered most. And how often do all of us get so caught up and distracted by all the serving and sacrificing we do that we forget only one thing is essential?

It's the middle of the night, and I'm reminded: when Jesus says he's the Main Course, it's not a suggestion about how life ought to be, but a statement about how life is. I'm reminded that consuming the Main Course is the key for making earth-life like a slice of heaven. Ordinariness is reimagined from our place on the floor next to Jesus. And at this frustrating juncture I needed to hit the ground, drape myself over Jesus' feet, and look up from there to get a level head so kingdom alchemy—this turning of mundane moments into miracles—can again become an intimate component of my parenting.

I was reminded of Martha and Mary during a groggy-eyed, middle-of-the-night bathroom break. And the next thing I knew I was hearing that the solution to all my dried-out days and mothering woes was the curving over, bent-to-serve, scrubbing of my own self . . . while washing the feet of my children.

Wash their feet. It was one of the most distinctive sentences to ever come silently to my mind, and immediately in the wake of the Spirit-words came a sense of rightness and holy reverence, a virtual lightbulb. Of course I would wash their feet. Why hadn't I thought of it sooner?

I had become so Martha-like about my days and tasks and especially about my kids, and I now knew that going low again and cultivating a Mary-like desire for heaven would be the breakthrough I needed to make magic from my mundane. I needed to see again that eternity was going on here and everywhere, and I was to bring continuity between right now and kingdom come by dipping into the bathwater and boys and lists and laundry with the intention of an alchemist.

I drifted back to sleep and knew that the foot-washing was going to change everything. And by "everything" I mean me.

A few hours later I was expectantly humming my way through the house gathering supplies—collecting bowls and bath salts, pumice stones and apricot scrubs, lotions and towels, my boys, and the Bible. Kingdom was coming, and the whole preparation felt in my soul like the chords of an old, favored hymn being sung by a choir of hundreds up in the rafters of a great stone-walled cathedral—soothing and voluminous, hallowed and tectonic, afire with divine mystery.

When I finally bent before the three young forms that I had fostered inside my own flesh and fed with my own umbilical blood, it didn't surprise me one iota to feel a heavenly hush descend over our heads and blanket the room in Artisan-made velvet. Every bone in my body went soft like warm wax, and my mouth couldn't speak above the barest breath of a whisper, and tears were already choking my throat, clumping my lashes, spilling from my eyes.

I opened *The Message* (my favorite translation) and read a Scripture story—not about Mary or Martha but about Jesus washing his disciples' feet. Then I spoke to Gabe, Seth, and Jude about a few things I understood the cherished narrative to mean and also how a finite person can only stretch and wonder at such an event, but never fully know the gigantic layers of meaning and ornamentation it holds.

Besides all that, I told them that my one, wild desire was to baptize this foot-washing sacrament with the kind of humility and love and passion Jesus showed thousands of years ago when he angled his legs and arched his heart before the dust-born bodies of his own hand-knit children.

Reaching for the first foot of my oldest son, I began the slow caressing and rhythmic massaging of his skin. And no sooner did I have his toes between my sudsy palms than we were all transported through ages and space and land to a long-ago upstairs supper room. I went down on my own knees in front of my kids, and before I knew what was happening we were there, wrapped and floating like dust dots, dancing within the Palestinian walls and next to the cosmic mystery of a slave-King bent and bowed, scrubbing miles of dirt from the pedestrian foot cracks and toenails of his subjects. Kneeling before them as if they were monarchs themselves.

And here I was in my own respective time, folded over and fighting the dark things inside me with a pair of feet between my massaging fingers. My eyes could see again and always that the way to find the light is to take on the status of servant and make a sacrifice of yourself on the altar of Jesus' famous "Follow me." He is always the way, the way of heaven on the way to heaven. And I never feel more like my true self than when I am bucking the current to walk in his steps.

When I lifted my tear-filled face to stare into my son, I would like to think that in the depths of my brown eyes he could see a Love that was older than extinction and longer than black holes and countless epiphanies. And while I held his feet between my hands, I would tell you that my own skin brushed softly past a few calluses of the One who logged so many dusty miles a few thousand years ago. Gabe and I became Jesus to each other through the unseen yet spellbinding enigma of the Who that sits between a bowl of water and a spectral anomaly.

Three times we did it, my boys and I, each washing as sacred as the last and as meaningful as the next. The bustling planet outside our four walls disappeared into a vortex of somewhere else. The One who once spoke peace to howling winds and waves now made the clock stand still, just so I could be fully present in a moment that had the power to metamorphose a heart. And the sweet, shining voices of my boys kept exclaiming that they felt like kings and they couldn't believe I was doing this for them and "Oh, man! This feels *so* good, mama!" And I said the sincerest "Amen" ever voiced because I could feel the arms and legs of the Holy Ghost fused with my entire body.

Together we had gathered the molecules of spirit from the air between our drywalls and door frames and gathered the molecules of spirit from inside my lungs and blood and brain. She had moved me around the house in a slow waltz while we gathered our base and mundane materials. We had mixed our media—the stuff of heaven (alchemy, spirit, air) and the stuff of earth (water, soap, fragrant oil)—and we had poured our gathered-up stuff into a basin so we could actually feel it, smell it, taste it, touch it on the feet of our children.

I haven't been the same since that supernatural stroke of time, and maybe never will I be the same again. My husband and I have washed our kids' feet several times since, and even when we don't reach for the actual bowl of water and bath scrub, the metaphor reminds us to go low in our approaches and postures in dealing with the boys. It reminds us to reach for a Mary perspective, to remember only one thing is essential. We return again and again to being present so we can experience Presence because it's salvation to be together with the One our souls long for.

Our family actively participates in this alchemic relationship with heaven's invisible qualities, even when the process feels gritty and arduous. Sometimes the boys are too busy and we parents are too tired and none of us feel like it. But we show up anyway because sometimes in the midst of so much parenting that smells like daily grind and elbow grease, a mama and a papa need to be governed less by what they feel ("Give me a break") and more by what they value ("Follow me"). We've measured the amount and have chosen to present our holy ashes for the purposes of alchemy anyway because we want to be rebel champions of impossible stories.

What would it look like if you were to reimagine the ordinariness of your own life as a stage for alchemy?

Are there ways that you could invite your children—or someone you live close with and care about—into a ceremony that intentionally celebrates the joining of heaven and earth?

She is always now and here and everywhere, this relentless Friend showing up in our midst. And when we least expect it—or even when we *do* expect it—she inspires us to breathe her hallowed breath so that we can go out into our ordinary world again and again and carry out her sacred work.

Let us believe in the alchemy of that breath, cling to its worth, and take the time to come together in love. Let us dare to make something new (or transform something old) out of the most base substances you might have in your bathroom cupboards or kitchen fridge or inside your own living organs.

Do you want to try this at home?

Do you want to caress the cosmic air between your fingers and get down on your humble, bent appendages and hug the atmosphere with every last little atom of your gifted existence?

Do you want to nurture your lovemaking with the divine, your holy union, and experience heaven all the way to heaven?

Dearly beloveds, we are gathered around this book today to learn or relearn or be reminded or reaffirmed that the stuff of heaven only waits for the sons and daughters of the earth to decide when they want to say "I do," get joined in holy matrimony, and embark on the most extravagant and intimate love adventure in all the known and unknown universe.

Wed the divine for Christ's sake. Make love, and don't stop until kingdom comes. There is no sky that limits this alchemic joining. This is gold refined . . . and redefined.

10

MEETING JESUS AT FROYO WORLD

I hope by now you feel inspired to look for alchemy in new and different ways, in unheard or unthought-of places. The stuff of heaven cannot be contained or localized; it is everywhere, happens anywhere. There is no place on earth where God cannot be found, and he will go to fathomless lengths to meet with you, mix with you, make with you.

Open your interior perceptions to this vast horizon of heaven within you and around you; explore any unexplored territory.

Observe the ordinary and perceive it with a breadth and depth that often gets missed.

Look beyond the human and behold the divine.

Always now and always here is when God is happening. Being an alchemist means you notice the unnoticeable in your everyday occurrences and connections and transmute the celestial into something seeable and touchable to the world at large. Imagine again what kind of beautiful can burst forth from the flesh and dirt and imagination of a mystical union when you purpose to totally lose yourself within the atmosphere of alchemy.

Across every spectrum and through every sphere of society we need virtuosos of kingdom alchemy who will go wide and high in their love of bringing heaven down to earth. This is how we make the Father visible.

Do you believe it?

Do you love the uncontrollable and audacious nature of a God who will come to us in unusual ways and when we least expect it?

Speaking of "unusual ways and when we least expect it," the boys and I found out one day what it might look like for Alchemy to move beyond our four walls, intersect with our city, and become an idea worth multiplying.

Watch this:

We were having morning meditation, and on this particular day there was an unusual burning in the Spirit. And before we registered what was happening, all of us were on our feet, crying and praying big ol' charismatic-y prayers against the grey walls of our living room. When our lips finally buttoned up after the heaven-bound supplications, we realized that something had occurred behind the veil, and the four of us circled together with a thirsty urgency to respond somehow, some way to what God was doing inside our skin. It felt clearly like we were supposed to *do* something, an outward movement, so I asked my guys, "What is one more thing we can do as a family to spread love, maybe one more thing we can do that would help ease the suffering of this city we live in?"

And suffer this city does, especially where we make our home on the rim between the prestigious empire of Yale University and the poorest neighborhoods of New Haven, Connecticut. In our neighborhood we consistently come face-to-face with the disinherited and devastated—what some people might call outsiders or misfits, including the prostitutes at the river park and the men and women panhandling at the corner grocery store. The need and despair presses hard into our daily lives and boldly challenges our faith, demands our rubber to meet an actual road.

We tried our hand at alchemy in the morning, and the boys came forth with a response that would invite cocreative magic. They decided just then that every time we went to the grocery store we should make a one-bag collection of good and fun food items to drop off to a homeless person, "to show them that they're loved and special."

Easy enough, I thought—one more bag of groceries each time we shopped for our own bounty. And it didn't seem like a time for my mama brain to analyze the sustainability or practicality of what their little hearts wanted to do. It was just a time to respond to a moment and to be present for their desire to donate from the overflow of our gifts and see if multiplication by sharing is, in fact, threaded through the laws of the universe as the gospel story of loaves and fishes suggests.

So we did it. We went to the Elm City Market on a Tuesday, and the boys pushed their own cart alongside mine, filling a bag full of love-picked edibles. On our way home we drove the few extra blocks to the center green and prayed to find a person who might need to feel noticed or special that day. And no sooner had the prayers left our mouths than we saw her—a homeless woman sitting on a park bench with her whole life stuffed in the big, exhausted bag between her legs.

"That's her," I whispered. We eased up to the curb, got out, and came alongside her shelterless shoulder. We looked into her eyes and asked if she could use some groceries. She had a bandaged wrist, and she smelled as bad as my own sin, but her tears were quick and her gratitude profuse. We walked back to the car with consuming emotions, slid in, and drove away with the convinced sensation that we had just fed Jesus. And Jesus had just fed us.

And it made me think about how vulnerable he must feel sometimes—when he comes to us in the form of a hungry human, puts his heart at our mercy, and wonders if we're going to feed him—knowing that we can always turn him down.

We can turn him down, or we can dive right inside him with a few bold prayers in the morning and a bag of groceries in the afternoon and an ongoing determination not to miss out on the opportunities to be kingdom alchemists, stirring the holy into everything we can think of.

To simplify it even further, here are the ingredients we used that day: (1) a commitment to availability and awareness; (2) a lust in our bellies to weave gladness and love and other fruit-like things into the fabric of our city, state, and universe; (3) a pocketful of bold prayers; (4) a "bag of groceries." And the result was magic, like any miracle story the Gospels have to offer.

Wherever you might be, whatever your ordinary ingredients or base materials, what are some ways you can apply kingdom alchemy to the life around you?

On the same day that we gave the bag of groceries away, I dropped the boys off to their downtown art classes and asked myself what I should do with my small window of kid-less time. My taste buds quickly made the decision for me: Froyo World (my favorite). And the next thing to slide across my conscience were these four simple words: *Take someone with you.*

I didn't take time to speculate about how this was going to happen. I just whispered an "okay," threw my gearshift into drive, and took the few minutes during the car ride to pray more or less the same prayer my boys and I had prayed earlier: *If there is someone who needs to feel seen or special or just might like some cold frozen yogurt on a hot day but can't afford it, then lead me to know who that person is.*

With the petition still warm on my lips, I parallel parked on High Street, unfolded from my seat, and commenced down the sidewalk toward my treat destination. A block or so before the entrance, I saw an old bum shuffling his feet in my direction. And the next few moments seemed to happen in slow motion as my spirit immediately reached for a Reality larger than my own, connected . . . and released a silent vibration from the recesses of my soul: *Oh my goodness, that's the one.*

I felt a little nervous, a small fear that I would be rejected for asking, but there was bliss in my belly too. We had showed up and presented ourselves for alchemy that morning, and God had taken us for his vessels; we had made love once already that day. Now here I was again, about to cross paths with a homeless man right in front of the door to Froyo World.

Before he could move past I put on my most genuine, beaming smile and made the invitation: "I'm going to have some yogurt. Can I get you some?" And this destitute-dressed man with the long, white beard meeting the middle of his red-and-black plaid–clad chest lit up like a moonbeam had burst open inside his near-toothless head.

"Well, *sure*," he affirmed and nodded for good measure.

Together we walked past the wide-eyed stares of Yale students and civilians. I handed him the biggest cup available, and he piled frozen yogurt as high as his container could bear and heaped on colorful mountains of fruit and candy. Side by side we took our cups to the counter, and while I was making the payment, I watched this beautiful, bedraggled stranger bite back his own nerves. Turning his soul-windows to search mine, he asked, "Would you like to sit and eat with me?"

And right there in the middle of Froyo World, with a dozen people silently watching our exchange, I stopped just long enough to search for the deeper meaning of the moment. Time stood still, and I felt myself both a participant in the scene and a spectator above it—as if I, too, were watching to see what was going to happen.

I could hear the cars driving by outside and see the pedestrians making their paces on the sidewalk and the employee standing behind the counter waiting, it seemed, for my answer. The whole host of everything was holding a collective breath. What would she say? What would she say? What would she say? I knew the Alchemist was waiting for my answer too. Would I accept the invitation to taste and see heaven?

Here I was in this suspended scene wanting to fall flat to my face and cry my happy heart out because I knew that I knew that I knew that Jesus was asking me to eat yogurt with him. And what I said past the tears ascending my throat were the same words this old guy had just said to me a few minutes before: "Well, *sure*."

I know what Augustine DiNoia means when he says "People behave as though God has gotten lost, and we must send out search parties to find him."[1] I behave that way too, as if God is the one who is absent or missing, when really my vision is so cluttered I can't see he's been in the next-to-me place all along and all the time—in my neighbor, in my kids, at the carwash or at Starbucks.

So we found our seats outside the Yale Center for British Art and savored our dessert, enjoying the companionship and sharing stories. "Joe" told me some whoppers, made me laugh, and near the end asked how old my husband was. "Make sure you don't tell him about our date," he said with a touch of mischief. I gave him a covert wink, a smile that couldn't quit, and a promise that this not-illicit rendezvous would be our secret.

I know what you've heard about Jesus—that he was Jewish, so naturally he had dark eyes and olive skin and a sturdy, carpenter nose. But I sat on a curb with Jesus that day, and he had blue eyes, a wicked sense of humor, sixty-five years' worth of wrinkles, a few crumbled teeth. And we ate frozen yogurt together like there was no yesterday or tomorrow.

I like to think that Joe found Jesus in me as much as I found Jesus in him—and isn't it wild to think of all the Jesuses we have yet to encounter—all the Jesuses that are literally around every street corner? All we need are the two open eyes and the two open ears of an alchemist, just enough looking and listening to see and hear what we can remake from the Spirit blowing in our direction and the stuff we're already doing anyway. Our lives reflect a picture of what we become, what the world becomes, when we allow alchemy to transform something, anything. A situation or . . . us.

After our encounters with the homeless Jesus on a park bench and the homeless Jesus at Froyo World, the boys and I decided we would adopt a revolving family member. We call him/her our "plus one." Now every time we go food shopping at Elm City Market or buy yogurt at Froyo World or coffee at our favorite cafe or dinner at the Noodle House, we purchase one more to give away.

It's just one bag or one meal or one treat at a time. But I have heard this Bible story about how a very small amount of food was shared, and through that sharing, multiplication-magic happened and thousands of hungry people were sustained.

What we're doing doesn't take the necessary place of soup kitchens or food pantries, but it offers something those institutions can't—an individual, face-to-face, special experience for one person. An opportunity for one man or woman to be seen and feel noticed beyond their obvious brand as "homeless."

Not once has our plus-one practice been convenient. On our good days, we take it on willingly, consciously giving up convenience to be Christ's embodiment. Some days, to be honest, we're a little grumpy about it, and sometimes the recipients are grumpy too. But every plus-one adventure I've participated in has been worth the trouble because we've communed more intimately with the person of Jesus than we ever have before—touching his hands and side, seeking his eyes, breaking his bread. "My beloved is mine, and I am his" (Song of Solomon 2:16 NKJV).

Let's go far together and be lovers, before we forget why we are here in this crazy place. My brothers and sisters, let's go far together and see all the bright things that can happen when we believe that alchemy is whirling in the wings of our everyday moments, just waiting for us to walk in and say, "I'm here, take or send or use . . . me."

We are the vessels by which alchemy manifests in our neighborhoods and cities and street corners, and sometimes all it takes is a tiny, quiet wait . . . just a still moment that's long enough for us to empty ourselves and open up to loaves-and-fishes possibilities all around.

It takes muscled determination to continually show up and declare to heaven that we are committed to cocreating alchemy yet again today and tomorrow, too, if we can muster the strength.

Whether it involves supplies that look to be nothing (potatoes? finger paint? dust bunnies?) or people society has labeled "nothing," our commission is to cooperate with Spirit to reveal the alchemic truth of their great value.

Remember, it's the lowly things of the world that Jesus spent most of his time on—from a despised, wee little man named Zacchaeus to a harlot from the hood to the basket of bread in the arms of a poor boy. He revealed that the worth of an entire real kingdom was inside the little things, and he redefined wealth accordingly.

Every day, we have the privilege to go and do likewise.

11

WHERE WAS SOMEBODY?

You must know by now that I am not saying anything particularly new. *Alchemy* is a word and concept that I've appropriated for the purpose of creating fresh ways of expressing and understanding what for some of us may have become tired or stale.

Do you find it to be true that some of our faith-tradition phrases have become clichés that chafe against the absolute glory and living synergy that is the triune God, revealed by and in the divine person of Jesus Christ? I do. So I went out with my empty basket and filled it with borrowed letters from the dictionary, deciding that certain ones would do for my usurping purposes. In these chapters I've attempted to cross these terms over, to nuance them freshly for the kingdom's sake. To strip Jesus of what I think are weary idioms and adages that seem to cling to the skin of him like the barnacles on our neighbor's oyster boat.

Does this sound too bold to you, or does it smack of arrogance? I am bold, I suppose, but I dearly hope I'm not arrogant. What you see here is simply my soul trying to stay true to my own lovemaking with the Spirit and to keep following Jesus, who also took the terms of his day and redefined them for the greater kingdom purpose. Take a look at how he did it, as interpreted through the blue-eyed lens of Frederick Buechner:

> If the world is sane, then Jesus is mad as a hatter and the Last Supper is the Mad Tea Party. The world says, Mind your own business, and Jesus says, There is no such thing as your own business. The world says, Follow the wisest course and be a success, and Jesus says, Follow me and be crucified. The world says, Drive carefully—the life you save may be your own—and Jesus says, Whoever would save his life will lose it, and whoever loses his life for my sake will find it. The world says, Law and order, and Jesus says, Love. The world says, Get and Jesus says, Give. In terms of the world's sanity, Jesus is crazy as a coot, and anybody who thinks he can follow him without being a little crazy too is laboring less under a cross than under a delusion.[1]

Jesus, in other words, detonated the dictionary. He turned heads and tables. He flipped familiar words and systems and ideologies in the service of true Truth. *Losing, gaining, wisdom, foolishness, law, love*—through history and on into eternity, every letter has been reshaped by his coming and his cross. *Alchemy* is no exception.

Alchemy is what I see when I look at the disciplined love affair between Jesus and the Spirit as scribed in the Gospel accounts. I believe that same connection is available in the same way, always and everywhere, to us the people—we are forever God's beloved. But it takes nothing less than all we've got to keep arriving at our own sacred marriage bed without contaminating the sheets with philosophies we've made from our own selves.

Because it takes both discipline and ardor to resist the seduction of contrary evidence the world slams in my face every day, I keep showing up to the back porch of my river house in the wee dawn of every spring and summer morning. I rock in my chair until all the prayers are pushed out through the cracks of my humanity and until I perceive the ineffable, transcendent Other through my intuitive connection with the Spirit. This cannot be had or seen or tasted with reason. There is a time to turn off the spinning mind and just exist in the conscious now, naked and whole.

We are always and fully—gloriously, like a full-bodied resurrection—enveloped in the living, vibrant, blazing presence of the Spirit. What we lack is the awareness to connect with her and feel the Wind on our skin, in our palms, stuffed in our pores and pockets. For the love of the kingdom and all things holy we have to teach ourselves how to see, become born again like babies and look with new eyes.

We were born seeing, then were conditioned by customary culture to sleepwalk. Jesus is the antidote to sleepwalking. "Stay watchful," he urges us. Invest in the health of your vision. "When your eye is healthy, your whole body is full of light" (Luke 11:34 ESV).

Do you make a habit of intentional alchemy? Do you go somewhere, anywhere quiet and slow to meet with a Lover and actively participate in the full presence of God? Find a porch swing or a dark closet or a patch of dirt in the backyard, and ask for sight and awareness. Inhale the molecules of Spirit and open your eyes like you've never seen the world before. Have a date and ask.

When you have a one-on-one with the Alchemist, you just may find yourself part of a story of changing lead into kingdom gold.

I was sitting cross-legged and so relaxed in the cracked leather chair at my favorite cafe, sharing lunch and meaningful life with a good girlfriend. We were talking in circles and spades, and our subjects ranged from triumphs to struggles to wave after wave of hard weather and the gale force of grace. Every now and again, between the sentences that spilled from our souls, I would shift my neck, glancing out the window at the next customer coming through the entrance. And right in the middle of the fourth or fifth shared story I saw a woman coming down the sidewalk.

She looked like crack-hacked riffraff with her torn clothes and stringy blond hair and half-gone teeth, and tears were raining in sheets down her cheeks. She was incoherently yelling—and I do mean yelling—out some bone-deep pain, as if the concrete was her confessional. Her entire body was visibly wracked with sobs—up and down, up and down.

I didn't even think a thought before jumping up from my seated spot. Releasing a small cry of "Oh, no. Hold on a second!" I launched out the door and rushed to her side.

She looked like the kind of woman who doesn't have hope behind her eyes or a belief in innocence or winning tickets or good luck for the weary and distressed—that is, for people like her. She looked like she'd seen too much, done too much, been used too much, like everything under the sun on this whole wide globe was just too much. Her drooped-down shoulders were less than halfway as high as they should be—arched over like someone's great-great-grandmother with osteoporosis. One of her hands clenched in a tight fist against her chest, as if her aorta had ripped and she was trying to hold the blood in before all her life force spilled out.

I've pictured it since and put myself in her tough shoes: *She's got nothing going for her. Nothing. She can hardly chew her food.*

"Dear God, who broke this woman?" I asked myself as I ran to her. I wanted to cut myself open and hold her inside my own warmth and wholeness. I wanted to say, "Here here here here—oh my God, here! Take some of my own red and white cells; I have millions more than I need." But instead I opened myself another way just by looking long and with love into her heavy-laden eyes and choosing to feel the labor of her weary breath; I wanted to share a yoke that was easy and born of Light. Her features were hardened and haggard, like a hike around nine thousand abusive blocks, and her limbs were ball-and-chained to the circumstances that brought her to her own walking death, but I could still see the fathomless, dark eye-pools of one singular incarnation within her face as easy as turning my gaze to the risen Son.

This woman needs clay vessels delivering the whole truth and nothing but the truth that she has always had Love's heart. Will she believe it if enough strangers unabashedly embrace her out of the blue and speak this wordless gospel through a flesh-to-flesh and spirit-to-spirit communion? (I'll hold somebody—anybody—I won't be afraid. We're all family anyway.)

I came right up next to her sobbing side, put my arm around her to hush-hush her like a baby being rocked, and rushed through three sentences at once: "Are you okay?" (Obviously not, but this is what you say.) "May I help? Do you need anything?"

Her response was to cry harder, and coming up on the heels of my desire to support came two of her equally bedraggled and gasping girlfriends. They told me they had been chasing this drained lady around the city. On top of everything else—homelessness and hopelessness and hunger and the like—she had just had a terrible fight with her "boyfriend." So I held her a little tighter and lifted her stoop with my own straight back.

I love you, my desperate darling, like you're mine, because you are.

I hugged her for only a moment, but everything in me went into that embrace. Then one of her friends stepped in. "Thank you so much. I didn't know people did what you just did. We'll take care of her now."

"Okay, are you sure?" I said. "Let me know if she needs anything . . . I'll be right in there." And I went back to my lunch, interrupted.

Within minutes, the same friend walked into the cafe to find me, and coming up to our table she spoke a few halted, high-emotion words: "I just want to thank you again for what you did." And the next sentence she spoke I will never, ever, ever in all eternity forget:

"Where was somebody when I felt that way every day for three months?"

Where was somebody?

Where was somebody?

Where was somebody?

My Jesus, where are all the somebodies for the whole globe of hurting people?

Still leaking metaphorical cells from my porous body, I made for home and went up to my bedroom to curl in a ball. And there in the quiet and calm I was reminded of something from my back-porch meditation that same morning, long before the lunch date and the street lady.

Sitting in my rocker with a cup of tea between my hands and my vision fixed on watching the river flow, I had begun praying words that had my eyes crying in no time flat. I'd told Jesus very specifically that I wanted to hold him today. Simple as that—"I want to hold you today." And I hadn't been talking about the way I hold my children or my husband or my friends.

That Jesus-holding is a daily given. That day I'd felt a hunger to hold Jesus in the specifically hurting, hungry, or hopeless.

Before I could remember that I had prayed that prayer, I'd found myself on a downtown New Haven sidewalk with my arms around a stranger who looked just like Jesus to me, who had all the features of the One who came for the sick and the poor and the disowned. And I had held him fast and true, like my life depended on it.

I thanked him so much for taking me at my word. Because being Somebody for Someone—I don't know how to describe the wholeness of it. Two broken people cling together on the streets, and suddenly the whole sky is split with shimmers.

I was Somebody for Someone. I was Jesus to Jesus, and Jesus was Jesus to me. Do you understand that? He and I are whole together.

It can happen for you too. All you have to do is get up in the morning or open your mouth during lunch or dinner or whenever and ask. Just ask to mix your particles with heaven, and magic can happen. It happens all the time.

Transmutation is on the tip of your tongue. Ask!

This is how the blind of the world, including ourselves, will begin to see the true kingdom again. This is our today-way of multiplying loaves and fishes. This is how our own drinking water turns to wine. This is how we see him and smell him and hear him and touch his side for ourselves if ever we've had a Thomas doubt.

Alchemy, remember, is "any magical power or process of transmuting a common substance, usually of little value, into a substance of great value." But kingdom alchemy reaches further and higher, refining and redefining.

The kingdom alchemist is fundamentally a lover of the Spirit, a person who learns to be awake to the undeniable Presence inside and outside of him or her—the One continually speaking and affecting and moving. The kingdom alchemist is willing both to listen and to act, to receive and to engage, all for the sake of kingdom come.

And now is the time. Now is always the time.

"Follow me" means trailing him into the miraculous world of kingdom alchemy right now. Eternal things do not have to wait, and you and I are the limbs and leaves and guts and keys to pulling heaven down around our ears for the sake of revealing our Father who dwells in celestial places, hallowed be his name. As the apostle Paul reminds us:

> God's Spirit beckons. There are things to do and places to go! This resurrection life you received from God is not a timid, grave-tending life. It's adventurously expectant, greeting God with a childlike "What's next, Papa?" God's Spirit touches our spirits and confirms who we really are. (Romans 8:14–16)

So open yourself up to alchemy and imagine all the places you'll go, maybe to the gutter or the trenches, which I'm told are actual heaven locations on earth. Maybe to the library or the market or the coffee shop, which are full of somebodies too. Imagine all the people you can touch, maybe someone you didn't even think you could feel with your fingers this side of the grave.

The alchemist is fundamentally a lover of the Spirit, a person who learns to be awake to the undeniable Presence inside and outside of him or her—the One continually speaking and affecting and moving. This intimate relationship with God is not only within your reach and inside your next breath but also your birthright.

Do you believe it?

Anthropology

12

REDEFINING ANTHROPOLOGY

Sometimes I lie in bed during the night watch and imagine all kinds of people standing behind my eyes. I purposefully place them there just so I can look long into their soul-windows and speak these words over them in the dark: "I see you."

Because what if nobody ever tried to see those before and my looking at them with love is like a prayer going out to cover and balm this most essential human need? They are not alone and you are not alone and I am not alone; we are shaped to see each other.

So I lie with my physical eyes shut and my spirit eyes wide open, and I reach my fingers forward to imaginatively touch all the men and women and children, grandmothers and old-timers, and I feel the panorama of skin colors and heights, sizes and shapes, hairdos and hineys. But more important, I see that all are carrying the weight of their own histories—an entire world riding piggy on each back. They're all fighting their own battles, wearing their own scars, bleeding from their own wounds, pushing through their own struggles.

We've all got chains and walls and masks and metals.

We're all haunted by devils and ghosts and lies and losses.

I see that you and you and all of you are bent with your own heaviness, just like I'm doubled over with mine. I see humanity has seven billion different molecular codes informing their responses and reactions, comebacks, knee jerks, wisecracks—persuading the spectrum of their emotions and decisions.

I see the guy who seems whole on the outside—his features are symmetrical and his clothes are pressed just so and his teeth are advertisement white—but his soul limps half-cocked like a zombie, diseased and mostly dead.

I see the one in the dark-alley shadows who perpetuates unspeakable evil, and I look at him extra long, taking the time to trace his life backward in my imagination with the hope of understanding what happened to him. "Who hurt you?" "Who didn't love you well?" I will always ask, and my eyes will be soft and my heart will bleed. (*Vagabond, come home.*)

I see the girl who thinks she's got it all figured out; she's got answers out the wazoo and confidence in loads, but really she doesn't have it all together, and sometimes she doesn't even know Jack. Sometimes that girl is me.

I see the religious and nonreligious, educated and uneducated, rich, poor, young, and old. I see the preposterous, vulgar, timid, boisterous, abused, broken, numb, bloodshot, drunk, diseased, depressed, drugged, and dumb. I see sinners, saints, sojourners, successes, eccentrics, bullies and bullied, straights and gays, clowns, misfits, fools, and thieves—all a mysterious mix of characteristics, a cocktail of spirit and DNA and trauma and life lessons.

Close your eyes and visualize the scope and breadth and depth of humanity. Close your eyes and take a look through landscapes and time zones, cultures, traditions, and tribes—all seven billion of us with our own history and haunts and codes and charms.

Do you see them? Really see them for what they are—all made of stardust and an exhale of the Holy Ghost?

Are you prepared to be a kingdom anthropologist?

You probably know that anthropology is the study of people. Anthropologists study humankind and their works—cultural, social, and economic. You may also know that explanation vastly oversimplifies a complex word and profession.

But I don't intend to dig much more deeply into the scientific field (or fields) of anthropological study. What I want to do is what I've been trying to do throughout this book—to cross the word over to the other side of Jesus and explore what it can mean to the bandersnatch endeavor.

Jesus was the greatest anthropologist that ever walked the hills and highways of terra firma. It didn't matter if he was staring into the eyes of a harlot or a hick, a racketeer or a rabbi, a street sweeper or a Samaritan. When Jesus looked at people, he knew them as if they had been birthed of his own flesh and vitals. He knew them as if he had just tightened his core muscles and leaned his torso a little sideways and to the left, just so he could expand his spirit eyes and catch a vision of the history whirling for hundreds of years in the dirt behind their backs.

Do you look behind people, too, to catch a vision of their every life experience and circumstance without judging or assuming the worst, observing them with kindness and compassion, remembering they bear the image of God? This is the intention that informs a kingdom anthropologist's view—the assumption that there is always so much more to the story than the surface sights.

Jesus saw Nathanael under a fig tree and Zacchaeus in a sycamore and Mary Magdalene on her unclean knees and the adulterous Samaritan woman drawing water from a well, but none of these factors seemed to define them in his heart the way society had already labeled them—Jew, crook, whore, outcast. He saw . . . them. No wonder the woman at the Samaritan well hiked her skirts high past propriety and ran back into town and told everyone to come and see the man who knew everything about her.

Do you imagine that we are commissioned to do anything less than Jesus did? Aren't we, the Christ followers, marked especially for this kind of careful and compassionate observation?

Sadly it has more often been my experience that those in Christian subcultures actually prey on the weak and untouchables, the "sinners" and the screwups, rather than looking at them through the nonjudgmental eyes of a kingdom anthropologist.

When you are face-to-face with someone, any someone, open your senses and take an interior moment. Ask for the Spirit to come and touch you, guide you, help you see more than an inch in front of your nose. We are made to gaze at humanity with a love that is an eternity long and wide and high. Imagine the trails and trials of everyone you meet. This is who you are, how you must live, as a man or woman who claims Christ as King.

Now that we've looked a little at what anthropology is and what its crossed-over version might be, I'm going to take brazen liberties and open the whole thing up. Because to me, crossed-over anthropology is not just about how we relate and engage and view humanity, but also how we embrace every natural element on God's green earth—water, wine, wheat, fish, crosses, coffee, cloaks, mud, yeast, nets, glitter, glue, milk, mustard seeds, seas, trees, stars, sand, fire, kangaroos, and kisses.

Before we go any further, I'm aware that the prefix *anthro* refers to humanity, not glue or grass or musical instruments or mustard seeds. So I suppose that technically we should be calling this crossed-over idea something else. But I'm playing off the biblical truth that God made humans out of dust and the scientific reality that everything on the planet is composed of the same matter and energy. So I'm all right with keeping the *anthropology* word and tweaking its meaning a tad. I hope you are too.

If *alchemy* redefined encompasses on an elemental level all the stuff of heaven (Spirit, magic, miracles, Wind, air, chills, zest), then what I'm suggesting here is that *anthropology* encompasses on an elemental level all the stuff of earth.

If alchemy is the stuff of heaven suspended in the atmosphere drifting and lifting and coming between and within every earthly thing, anthropology is every earthly thing inspirited and made beautiful by the stuff of heaven.

Practically speaking, kingdom anthropology is a radical way of seeing everyone as if you've lived inside their skin and everything else for its full potential. When we approach this idea with the values of a vanguardist and the intention of an alchemist, then you get something like:

Bread is not just a loaf of wheat and yeast; it's the risen body of Christ. Wine is not just a glass of fermented grapes; it's the pressed and poured-out blood of Jesus. Combined with alchemy, anthropology becomes a transportation device taking us directly to the Last Supper . . . and this week's communion table.

And we can go on from there: It's not just a mustard seed; it's the kingdom of heaven.

It's not just five loaves and two fish; it's a meal for five thousand.

It's not just dirt and spit; it's mud to heal a blind man's eyes.

Jesus didn't bring in the kingdom of heaven without engaging the elements of earth—anthropology.

The kingdom anthropologist will always see the stuff of earth as an artery to the kingdom of heaven. The stuff of earth and the stuff of heaven were made for one another. Each gets us to the other.

Each gets us to the other.

So it's not just a bluebird mounting the wind against grey gossamer clouds; it's a silent Voice—the Great Mystery—trying to reach through to you and lift your heart again to where your help comes from.

It's not just a beggar burrowed under blankets and begging for bread; it's the actual incarnated flesh of Jesus waiting for you to touch him.

Alchemy and anthropology are designed to be inseparable, like soul and spirit. I'll say it again: Jesus always used the stuff of earth in conjunction with the stuff of heaven to reveal and bring his kingdom, to anchor his parables and his purposes.

On the other side of Jesus, anthropology is much more than a study of *Homo sapiens* and the hows and whats of human culture. It's basically a devoted interest and interaction with all the stuff of earth. And by "devoted interest and interaction," I mean such an arduous and audacious pursuit of the two that you hunt them down all the days and ways under the sun, hunt them down for all the days and ways the two can collide on this side of the grave. And you do it, of course, hot on the heels of Jesus.

"Follow me," he says.

Our neighborhood is a beautiful and brutal place, and for the intents and purposes of this story, I first need to focus in on the brutal bits. We've got contentious characters and gunshots and razor edges and half-clad prostitutes and drug dealers—a veritable swarm of the "ugly," tawdry, and downright dangerous that we walk through and around and are affected by day after day after week after month after—well, we've been here for more than twelve years now. Our streets and sidewalks and parks and gutters are littered with all kinds of trash. And the kind of trash that confronts us everywhere is way more, um, varied than the produce packages, food fragments, wrappers, and receipts that make up the average waste stream.

For example, this is one of two hundred thousand weird conversations I've had with our children since we've lived where we live.

> **Seth:** Eeeeeeeeew! Mama, what's that?
> **Me:** What? Oh, that. That's a used condom.
> **Jude:** What's a comdon?
> **Me:** Not comdon. Con-dom. It's something people use during intercourse when they want to prevent pregnancy or sexually transmitted diseases.
> **Jude:** What are sexually transmitted diseases?
> **Me:** I'll tell you when you're a little bit older than eight.

We talk straight in our family, and we've seen it all. The trash we encounter regularly ranges from fast food bags to dirty diapers to drug needles and crack sacks—plus random items like footed baby sleepers, garden hoses, TVs, treadmills, broken furniture, and bassinets with empty beer bottles inside. Sometimes we play a family game called "I Have Never Seen That on a Sidewalk Before"—and everyone wins.

Now, one of our deeply held family values is a kingdom-anthropology one—we believe we are called to tenderly care for the earth. So over the years we've periodically bought our boys protective gloves, armed them with garbage bags, and hauled their semireluctant butts on a number of local street-cleaning campaigns. But we have also had fairly long periods when we just don't get out there. We just get tired of picking up heedless people's debris only to have some other careless person replace the mess. It feels like defeat, and we run out of fight and get tired of tending the mess that isn't ours.

So that day we were sitting on the couch feeling convicted about not moving ourselves out the door to keep doing the good work when our cat, Louix, got into the act.

Now if Louix (more commonly referred to as Boofus) could deliver a five-point sermon—with bristled fur, flailing paws, and great preacherly gusto—I'm certain he would tell you all the reasons why his little feline heart is much more concerned with orthopraxy than orthodoxy. In other words, maybe he would say that values and beliefs don't mean a hill of Jack's beans unless you're putting motors where your mouth is.

How do I know what our purry pet would preach? Because I've caught his nonverbal sermon firsthand.

I was sitting on the patio the first time it happened. Louix came trotting from the woods next door, and he had a vile-looking, used plastic grocery sack hanging from between his feline teeth. Much to my bafflement, he dragged that thing all the way to my feet, stared straight into my face, and dropped it like an offering. Then he went back into the trees on the hunt for more garbage. In one day he retrieved two plastic sacks, an empty chip bag, and a McDonald's drink cup. And with each retrieval, he added to a nasty little pile next to me.

Maybe the cat knows something about kingdom anthropology. At any rate, he got my attention. And my mama, who's been religiously picking up garbage ever since she moved to New Haven, took this as a sign sent straight from Zion. She went out to buy our whole family "pickers" and five-gallon buckets.

Soon after that, armed with a backpack full of thirty-gallon trash bags and boxes of gloves, my mama and I planned an epic cleanup crusade. We plotted to spend an entire day with the kids scrubbing a one-mile stretch of street. Now, one mile doesn't sound like a big thing, but this particular area we chose was the worst of all the dirty places. It was high and wide and long, stacked and layered with fathoms and leagues' worth of junk. You can ask the locals. We were taking on quite the challenge.

The day dawned cool with autumn temperatures and colors, and we all met at the corner of Ferry and Chapel with our necessary gear. We had supplies galore, but I knew what we needed more than anything that day was a willing grace and nonjudgmental hearts.

Is trash still the stuff of earth, the realm of kingdom anthropology, and does the service of bending over again and again and again until your back and thighs and calves go screaming at you still hold the possibility for heaven to open the curtain and meet us? We believed it, so my mama and I turned to our boys and told them that the most important purpose of being anthropologists and alchemists was bringing heaven and earth together for a party.

We looked at them with fire burning inside us and told their young faces that each piece of wreckage we picked off the ground was invisibly connected to a person and that every single time we bent down to clean up, our prayers could lean in the direction of the human who unconsciously threw out his or her waste. We told our boys that the kingdom of heaven was in our hands today and we should not underestimate this seemingly mundane and thankless task. We invited them to understand how their humble generosity of time and service of love could actually ripple the spiritual fabric over our city and bring healing to the land.

And right there on the street corner, looking like Lord knows what to the traffic and passersby, we grabbed one another's hands and bowed our heads and said prayers. We invited alchemy to mix with all this anthropology and make something artful with it. We prayed that when our hands cleaned up the mess, it would make a difference in hearts. We prayed most that we would remember the Jesus who cleaned up all the messes he didn't even make.

And that's the point that pierced more than all the rest that day. In a small way, we stood beside Jesus and identified with something of his life. Cleaning up messes we didn't make turned out to be a gift boomeranging back around and knocking us upside the head, because that gift lassoed us into the side of the Savior and allowed our souls to share in his sensations and sacrifice.

After six nonstop hours of cleaning, we hoofed our tired trunks toward home. We couldn't help but notice that there was already more trash where we had just finished cleaning. And I couldn't stop the tears, the hurt, or my heart from breaking just a little bit. Chapel Street had just been wiped clean, and it had stayed clean for less than a New York minute.

Ah, this sounds familiar, says the girl in constant need of grace.

As I sent a prayer out to go along with my cuploads of cry, a reminder came in of a God who has never stopped cleaning my mess and that of billions of others—again and again and again and again—for thousands of years and until forevermore. Besides, living consistent with Christ's character; maintaining a value of "Follow me," means that I don't get to pick and choose the ways in which my feet chase after him. I just need to let my tread go in his direction come hell or high water and no matter what.

Continuing to choose Jesus and learning to follow him also means I continue to see from his vantage point. And God gave me this perspective that day: I learned not to see trash anymore, but instead the faces of my brothers and sisters. I learned not to see filth anymore, but huge heaps of grace.

Because of my active engagement with alchemy and my choice to be the kind of anthropologist I see in Jesus, filthy rubbish became a portal to paradise.

I want to take a section and bring it all together so far:

Is your body full of avant-garde and alchemy and the beginnings of anthropology? Have you begun weaving them betwixt your ribs and roots and fibulas and feelings? You're still gonna need some radical, unorthodox receptors and projectors and the fervent desire to mix ourselves with the stuff of heaven and the stuff of earth. So while you stop and scan yourself, let me say again: there is only one of you.

Who you are and the way you approach life and relationships and creativity and contribution will never be duplicated in another incarnation.

You were created by a diverse Designer; conformity is a human-made institution that keeps you from your original, unorthodox, or radically daring personhood.

You are allowed to arrive at life as your own weird and

wonderful self and push against the boundaries of what is accepted as normal or status quo. And you can extract the systems and self-defeating games and lies that keep the truth of you from organically blooming to life inside you.

If avant-garde is your lens, then walk into a moment and sit in holy silence—the holy voice of God—long enough to hear him teach you how to be an alchemist, transmuting your ordinary and common life and substances (the stuff of earth, anthropology) in a way that only you can. Mindfully access the stuff of heaven and open yourself to magic and miracles. And at the same time, try to see people, plants, and places—the stuff of the earth—in a way they've never been seen before, with untold possibility and unprecedented love.

Avant-garde plus alchemy plus anthropology—this is how the Baby gets born again into our world, when we offer ourselves to be heavenward transmuters of all the elements on the earth and earthly carriers of all the elements spinning within the sky. This is how salvation comes and cracks get healed and hope is not all lost. This is how streets get cleaned and our own smudged hearts are wiped. Kingdom come.

13

WHEN LOVE SMELLS LIKE SEVEN
YEARS OF UNWASHED SKIN

Without using the language of anthropology and alchemy or avant-garde, my mama inspired us to the nth degree with what it meant to be alive, destined to touch every particle of earth's stuff while simultaneously caressing the richness of heaven. When the two come together, Jesus happens. And if you have ever ached to press your palms to that broad and beautiful Nazarene face—his warm lips and eye lines and the vibrations of his laughter—this is the only way I have ever seen or heard of it being done since the Ascension.

I think my mama knew this. She loved Jesus something fierce, and she'd be dad-gummed if she didn't get to feel his features herself. And the best way she did it was through her caring and compassionate works with the invisible and untouchable groups of humanity—the ones Jesus comes to us in, the ones we can always turn down or turn against or turn away from. Mama excelled at drawing close to these least of Jesus' brothers and sisters.

I remember the first time she dragged our little homeschooled hineys to the local nursing home. She thought it would stretch our spiritual growth, develop our characters, benefit humanity and the whole globe if we went and emptied our love tanks on the lonely old folk. "They are a forgotten people group," she would say to me and my two siblings when we were seatbelted side by side in the back of the car on our way to Birchwood Nursing Center. And I was as eager as they come because my untried love for Jesus was bigger than my body could contain, and I wanted to share all the extra adoration that was practically spilling off my skin.

Giving care to the uncared-for sounded like such a good idea . . . until we got there.

I purposely say "until" because upon opening the doors to that poorly kept place, our senses were immediately offended by the most obnoxious wall of eye-watering odor. I couldn't even breathe half a breath without tasting the uncleanliness of it. The smell of excrement and urine hung in the air, and close second to the high stink came my very first visual on that very first visit: a shuffling, hunched-over great-grandfather dropped his drawers in the middle of the corridor and eliminated both bathroom numbers all over the floor.

I had never even seen or smelled such things in all my born days.

I must've looked like a deer caught in the headlights, so shocked was I, and when something finally snapped me out of my stupor, I wanted nothing more than to turn and run frantically for the hills of anywhere but there. This wasn't a pretty or happy or nice place—not even close. There were no flowers on the windowsills or rose-colored glasses being passed out when we walked in. This was the worst of the world that I had seen—gritty, harsh, and putrid. Being there felt like being inside a coffin.

A five-minute car ride from home, and we were standing and sniffing in the very margins of society. And being there suddenly felt like a portal into my untested soul, her small boundaries and weak capacity for love. I never knew I didn't have enough of the stuff until that day. Jesus had said, "Follow me," and I had eagerly said yes. But little had I known that following would take me to the noxious "home" of a forgotten people-group stuck in one location to watch the minutes tick down on their life clock.

I'll find another way to follow Jesus, thank you very much. My love was gasping and sputtering behind layers of nostril-clawing stench.

But when you're a kid, you don't get to make all the decisions for yourself. So for four and a half years my mom religiously conveyed us to that nursing home every Friday. Maybe she knew how much I needed to be transformed, how much I needed to learn of love. Maybe she wanted me to grip the face of God and grow from there.

Whatever her intention, that is what happened.

Sometimes gripping God's face would look like us gathering in the group activity room to play cards or bingo. Sometimes it would look like us setting up a "beauty parlor" so the ladies could get their chin whiskers plucked and hair set on rollers. (I didn't know Jesus liked his hair curled.) Sometimes it looked like us bathing our goats in the shower at home, tying bows around their necks, and bringing them to the nursing center for a makeshift petting zoo. Sometimes it looked like riding our horses there so the elderly could reach out their gnarled hands and savor the smooth, velvet feel of Trinka or Roman's snout against their wrinkled hands.

Sometimes we would bring a chicken or two to buck and cluck around the hallways. Sometimes we would go from room to room visiting one person at a time so we could learn from them and their exhaustive stories of love and war. Some were bitter; some were effervescent. Some yelled at us to "get out," while some couldn't get enough of our company.

So many of the individuals burned a permanent brand inside my young heart, an imprint that still informs who I am today—from "Queen Ruby" with her stark-white, royally coiffed updo to ninety-eight-year-old Harold, one of the last remaining World War I veterans, to mute Helen, whose eyes would go wild and angry if you happened to say "God" in the course of conversation. So in lieu of God, we brought our kitty. He would settle on her lap with a purr, and the most profound peace would fall over her face. It seemed that for Helen, God could only be found in the fur of a feline.

For four and a half years we told these men and women by our efforts and our energy that they were worthy.

For four and a half years they taught us how to agape love.

It was probably the most formative experience of my childhood.

By forcing those visits, my mama gave us one of the greatest gifts a parent can ever offer an offspring: the ability to be awake and engaged, on our knees in humility and awe before a world so alive and precious, so filled with hardship and pain it will make a person praise and weep all at once. She stood behind our growing bodies; lifted our faces to the horizon, to the very near Son; and told us to open our eyes. She invited us to look with the vision of an alchemist and an anthropologist and see, really see, how Spirit waited in the wings of every moment and around every earthly element, breathlessly hoping for us to make eternal magic with the commonplace and then infuse those same ordinary things with the breath of heaven. She was a brilliant teacher of truth, constantly curling our hands around people and stuff and our spirits around the Holy Ghost.

I can't talk about anthropology—this profound and holy relationship with humanity and the stuff of earth—without also remembering alchemy. Because without alchemy, without the Spirit-filled magic that turns lead to gold in our minds and hearts and our spirits, our intersections with the stuff of earth inevitably fall flat and lifeless.

Keep this in mind always: God made them to be married to each other for eternity.

The book of Revelation says that Christ is "coming soon" (22:20 ESV), and *soon* must be one of those relative terms because two thousand and more years later I haven't seen anybody come descending from the clouds.

But what if instead of waiting for Jesus to come soon, we decide to be channels by which he comes now? All this talk of alchemy and anthropology and the birthright of a vanguardist— surely you must know that it's all for one purpose: to show the million-times-infinity unique and peculiar and never-been-nuanced-before ways by which we can bring Jesus today. We can bring him right now to the dregs and mucks and roads and rigors of our lives without even waiting.

Do you believe it?

Have you thought about how it might happen?

I feel as though so many of our ways have grown tired—the ways of the church, the ways of tradition, the ways of the world. And here we are, the keys to God's continued creative work, standing between kingdom come and kingdom not yet come, in desperate need of fresh ideas for making the earth a domain that looks like the life and death of Jesus.

Are you getting some? Are you already beginning to imagine what it might look like for you to be an anthropologist, loving people and the earth with the same kind of madness that Jesus did?

The only way for kingdom to come now is for the kingdom disciples to invite and participate in acts and elements by which "on earth as it is in heaven" is made and brought in our every, ordinary day.

What else does "kingdom come" mean if not this turning over and redefining of the world's systems and rules and idioms and axioms? If one kingdom is going to come, then another kingdom must give way and recede in our lives, and we must do what it takes to make it happen.

This is not a sedentary experience; it takes an active determination and joy. So let's put our hands to the ground and begin sowing change, water the ashes that have been made of our own messed-up minds and machinations, and manifest a few new subtleties under the sun.

Having the eyes of an anthropologist has the potential to change not only us, but the sphere of society around us as well.

The homeless community in our city is the "nursing home" we drag our own kids to. I say drag, but really it's more like "Mama, Papa, there's Roger. I see Roger—he's over there. Hey Roger, Roger!"

Our boys are always excited to see him, like he's Christmas morning, a gift to be unwrapped—or like finally finding Waldo after you've been staring at the same scene for ages. On this particular day, it was a blistering ninety-eight degrees when we drove downtown and bumped into Roger on our way to get ice cream.

He was dressed from stem to stern in black and sweating down to his skeleton. He was particularly distressed that day, so I made sure to give him an extra huge hug, and it was still everything I could do to wrap my arms around him as if he didn't smell like seven years of unwashed skin. I struggled not to hold my breath when I leaned my nose in next to his weathered neck, where the worst smell sat in the shadowed, clotted creases. But I don't allow myself half-arsed hugs when it comes to our homeless friends, not when that embrace may be the only tender touch they receive for the week or whole year—depending on how lucky we get when we go to town. (Finding one particular homeless man in a city of more than 150,000 is totally the same as looking for a needle in a haystack.)

So I put everything meaningful in my arms as I squeezed him, squeezed him with all the Jesus that's now grown in me, and then stepped back. My formerly pristine palms came away wet with sweat, but I didn't care because I was looking deeper than the surface now, subconsciously inviting Jesus, the great Anthropologist, to show me his face even here in the heat of the day with the hot sun blazing and the humid air dripping. I chose awareness. I chose to be an anthropologist. I looked at the history trailing behind Roger's back; I looked in his eyes and asked about life.

Roger told us he had gotten "new" shoes, and I looked down to see holes in both toes. Maybe they matched the holes in his heart, the ones left gaping by the guilt he harbors from all the mistakes he says he's made, especially that long-ago decision to divorce his "crazy" wife and leave his little boy and girl in state care. "I wanted them to have a better chance than I could give them," he says, but his eyes always hold uncertainty.

It is never the time for an anthropologist to judge and decide what different choices a guy like Roger could have made—nobody knows the long list of red devils that have been preying upon a person. Every time is the time for us to eke out all the ounces of grace we can muster and pour them in a glass so Roger (or anyone else) can drink a cup of cold water on a hot day in the name of Jesus and for Christ's sake. Every time calls for an intentional decision to imagine ourselves wearing his world, because I believe it's the only way we can truly and fully love him.

With just a little zip from the top of his head to the flats of his feet, we can simply slip inside his skin. And it's *so* hot in here and we're trying to stand up under the weight of his sad times, trying to breathe through the unbearable humidity of his internal climate, but there isn't any air-conditioning there, where a tiny bit of hell is beating here between his bones. So we dip down to shoulder up his heart, putting our own aortas next to his just so he's not burning alive inside all alone.

Right alongside me, my husband and the boys threw their arms around Roger because this is how we do, and he became the center of our world for the next half hour. We bought ice cream and ate the odor of our companion with every bite, and it sure was hard sometimes to swallow it all down on the same spoon. But this is sustenance of body and soul, and when Roger told us what had been making him so sick recently, we had his back covered with arms of love and took turns praying and holding his hands like we were born to it. Because we were.

If anthropology is a radical way of seeing everyone like you've lived inside their skin and everything else for its full potential, then even when all we have to work with is a sweaty homeless man and the smell of excrement and the elderly—the most "common" and base of substances—these are still the elements by which we mix anthropology with alchemy and have a meeting with Jesus right now.

King Solomon says that "a good man leaves an inheritance to his children's children" (Proverbs 13:22 NKJV). I know he's referencing monetary wealth in that verse. But let me tell you this: The nonmonetary inheritance my mama passed down to me to give to my children is worth far more to me than all the dollars in Bill Gates's bank account. She gave us—and, consequently, her grandchildren—the inheritance of a kingdom anthropologist who earnestly practices kingdom alchemy, of someone who suspends assumptions and shows compassion and knows how to bend and give and stretch and spend energy to make heaven come in an earth moment.

Our sole purpose as kingdom anthropologists is to replicate Jesus, to interact with people and things the same way Jesus did. If he had never touched anybody or really seen them when he looked at their faces or responded with deep compassion, then he wouldn't have been Jesus at all. Doing those things—touching and seeing and loving—made him who he was. He touched people and made them whole. And those same people made him wholly himself because through them he taught us his purposes for the earth and her inhabitants.

For us to be who we are, we must go and do likewise.

We were born to cover each other, hold each other, need each other—the Rogers of the world and us. Being a kingdom anthropologist is not about going out and fulfilling self-serving acts so that we can feel good about ourselves. It's about being one, being whole, being a family, and being catalysts of love and healing back and forth. Do you believe that your wholeness is bound together with people who are not like you and may even be undesirable to you?

The world is wide open, a yawning chasm waiting to be filled with love that works like the hands and feet and warm blood of Jesus. Losing yourself in this work makes you grow and is essential to the soul of everything.

14

YOU MADE ME LOOK AT YOU

If we knew how afire with Holy Spirit every person is, we would run to the people we see and hug and hold on, even at the risk of looking like a lunatic. If we knew how afire with Holy Spirit the whole world is, we would know that we are never safe, that there is no place to hide from a God who will enter into any insignificant or ridiculous moment and burn it alive with divine purpose. Just when and where we least expect him is the place he would like to surprise us if only we open our minds and our senses wide enough to see.

In his book *The Hungering Dark*, Frederick Buechner writes:

Once they have seen him in a stable, they can never be sure where he will appear or to what lengths he will go or to what ludicrous depths of self-humiliation he will descend in his wild pursuit of man. If holiness and the awful power and majesty of God were present in this least auspicious of all events, this birth of a peasant's child, then there is no place or time so lowly and earthbound but that holiness can be present there too.[1]

The presence of God does not restrict itself to respect our limits. It is not discretionary or prejudiced and cannot be contained. And yet so often we (myself included) put conditions and prerequisites on how we imagine God should reveal himself, thereby missing out on myriad opportunities to intimately commune with him through the created order. This is what I'd like to address in this chapter, especially as it applies to other people.

If we let our assumptions and judgments about people, no matter how justified they seem, prevent us from seeing Jesus in men and women who are "other" from us, then we've bought into a society-originated system that says human value is measured by a man-made definition of worth or success or perfection or cleanliness or contribution.

We need to retrain our eyes to look past our cultural norms and narrow boundary markers to see the blazing glory of God in everyone.

Her name is Diamond.

By the time she was twenty-one, she had borne three children with three different baby daddies and been around her share of city blocks. Her eyes are deep brown, but not as dark as her thoughts most days. Her shoulders sag under the weight of ongoing drug abuse, failed relationships, and the guilt of neglecting her children. She's chosen her addiction over kissing her kids good-night. She can't kick the habit for the love of anything, even though she kicks herself to sleep every evening when she lays her head down on a different street corner or at the local bus stop, depending on the weather.

Diamond would give thanks to the Powers that be, if she believed in them, for the good looks that make her so successful at panhandling for money as well as selling the poems she writes on her wrist on the rare occasion when she's hit with inspiration. Maybe in five years (or never) Diamond will have just enough ounces of willpower to get straight and finish high school. Maybe in five years (or never) she'll be alive and clean enough to raise her own kids. Maybe in five years (or never) she'll have a job and live in her own home, as she always dreamed.

It will be either in five years . . . or never.

I know Diamond's story because she was standing in the spilling-down January rain outside the pizza parlor when we arrived with family and friends to celebrate our youngest son's ninth birthday. We were up on gaiety and togetherness, excited to make our little "Monkey" feel like five million Ben Franklins. Then Diamond showed up with her missing teeth and her swagger and inserted herself between our bodies to plead with my mama for money.

Of course, my mama did what I would've done if I'd gotten there first—she invited Diamond to our party. "Come to our table and eat with us," she said. Come into our laughter and love and joy-filled family energy; we've got enough to go around, and that includes you too. Come like you're hereditary, born of our corpuscles and codes and chromosomes.

Diamond didn't look this gift horse in the mouth. She enthusiastically accepted being swung into the rowdy and loud lot of us. After all, we were at Modern Pizza, voted third best pizza in the nation, and who would turn that down? So we waited together for our table, and while we waited I was getting to know her like she was my new best sister . . . because she was.

This is not a mystery to me anymore. Nobody is the sum of their circumstances, and on the other side of Jesus, everybody is my family. I'm a kingdom anthropologist, which means it's going to take an eternity to get to know all the people I'm related to.

So I always start with the one right in front of me.

Diamond told us that she had just gotten "out" from being "in" for thirty days. She had a crack-cocaine habit but hadn't planned on getting caught. Maybe her mama could have taught her better how to hide from the authorities if she hadn't died of an overdose on the same day Diamond gave birth to her first baby during her fifteenth year of life.

Life—now there's a relative term. Diamond was pushed slippery and small and already high on heroin into the arms of a drug-dealing daddy, raised under the volatile roof of addiction, and tucked to sleep each night—scratch that. Nobody tucked Diamond to sleep or sang her lullabies or smoothed her brow or kissed her cheek or told her that she was a one-and-only, unique, and specially created daughter with the Divine for a daddy.

A sad story—and yet Diamond was the life of our party, making jokes and being all sarcastically loud, messing with the birthday boy like she'd been his aunt for his whole life. "Jude, Jude, let me see your presents!" She was sitting next to me and reaching over the plates and pizza with the familiarity of intimate fellowship. I saw her God-given gifts underneath all the winter layers and the heavy makeup she wore like a mask, and without even thinking about it she was offering them into our fold.

In the quietness of my heart, I spoke important words over Diamond's broken body. *Come home with me, sister. I love you right here and right now. Come to the one true table. You are needed and wanted, and darn if you don't make the party better and the celebrators more whole. I see that you are afire with the flames of God, and I want to weep for you, beckon you with outstretched arms.*

What if we had passed by Diamond panhandling? We might have missed seeing someone as necessary as air.

Is befriending a homeless, child-abandoning druggie and showing love to her without insisting she change first a radical notion?

Shouldn't you be putting your own children's safety first?

Aren't you just enabling her lifestyle?

She's made her own bed; you should have left her to lie in it.

People like her are a waste of good, honest taxpayers' money.

Make her get her act together and then be her friend.

These are some of the voices I have heard from a society that bolsters the assumption that people like Diamond are a boil on the butt of the general public, that she drags the rest of us down.

But what if we really believed that Diamond isn't a deficit, but a necessary and vital link to the interlocking circle of contribution—not when she finally gets her act together (which might be never), but just as she is? Diamond didn't need to be anyone or anything else than what she was in order to touch my actual soul and bring change to my heart.

She was a gift the night I met her. She is a gift right now—in the same way that an unclean harlot woman was a gift to Jesus when she poured her life's savings over his feet, consecrating him for burial. He saw her for the gift she was right then, not for the gift she could be (see Luke 7:36–50). And the kind of love Jesus gave without any shoulds or conditions or prerequisites—the kind we give if we're serious about following him—is the most healing, transformative elixir known to the planet.

Diamond and people like her need to know their value and worth now, before enrolling in a twelve-step program or cleaning up their act. Her situation and circumstances and choices do not disqualify her from being a contributor or a woman with assets to share with the world. She is not a deficit to the global family for being dependent on drugs and handouts but is infinitely more than the things that have happened to her or the decisions she's made. Somebody has to keep telling her she's beautiful and bright. And above all the things I can think of, I just want to yell all the time: "Diamond, Diamond, you made me look at you, and now more than ever I want to see you shine."

I want to see her shine because she's a daughter of the Divine, but she's so used to handouts and hard living she doesn't believe there's anything left of her to gleam. Little does she know that hers is the face of Jesus, that we'll miss seeing him if we walk the other way. And we hide from her the face of Jesus in our own features when we choose not to look in her direction.

When I offered you an opportunity to unconventionally explore your peculiar soul, this is an included avenue to that process. You will not know yourself fully without welcoming people into your life who are not at all like you.

This, too, is how you come to learn who you are.

Through kingdom anthropology.

It took me a month of driving around the city streets, looking up and over and down the alleys and along the sidewalks, before I found her again.

My mama and I and the boys had been walking downtown to catch a matinee, and about three blocks from the theater we found Diamond loitering at the Chapel Street bus stop. (This particular place is like the homeless people's front parlor.) I was up ahead with the boys when I heard my mama yelling from behind me, so I turned around to see that she finally had

Diamond in her arms and a big beam across her face. "I found Diamond!"

And I swear to you that I heard the theme song to *Chariots of Fire* playing in the back of my brain as I ran to Diamond and pulled her body into mine and said, "Where have you been? We've looked everywhere for you. And how are you? And we've been getting so worried." She was even skinnier than the last time I saw her, which I hadn't thought was possible, but I'm thinking that three square meals a day and no drugs in jail had filled her out a little then. While living on the streets she divides her earnings between drugs, drink, and real sustenance.

Diamond was admittedly high as a kite that day from smoking dope and just as happy and uncoordinated as a pack of puppies on a playdate—weaving and slapping and speaking volumes louder than necessary. My mama asked her if she wanted to join us for the movie, and the loopy Diamond literally skipped across a road of oncoming traffic without looking so she could inform her "husband" (not actually her husband, but the guy who protects her when she sleeps on the benches) that she would be gone with us for a few hours. Then she skipped back across the road without looking at the cars or buses screeching around her, and Mama and I palmed our faces with both hands in a reaction of horror. People on drugs should not be crossing streets.

I had some curiosity about how a high Diamond would do in a movie theater. My question was answered as soon as we settled in our seats with popcorn and treats and Diamond spilled her whole bag of peanut M&M's on the floor. We could hear a hundred colored pieces of candy rolling down the theater slope while a blue streak of not-quiet cuss words came streaming out of Diamond's mouth.

I need to tell you at this point that Diamond is a world-class cusser. She's got curse words you haven't even heard before, and the way she slices certain ones apart, then glues them together differently, is truly impressive—you'll just have to trust me on this. My mama and I had to chuckle at her creativity even as we kept saying, "Diamond, shh." Between the boys and Diamond we probably met our "shh" quota for a whole month during the first thirty minutes of that movie.

Take it from me—if you are going to the movies to really invest in the screen time, you really shouldn't take someone with narcotics coursing through her veins. But that day with Diamond wasn't about the film we were seeing. That day was about a specific communion with common elements that would unite us to the Lover of our souls. That day was about Jesus showing up to us in the poor woman we didn't have to take in our arms and drag with us to the movies and buy candy for. But we did it anyway, and it was our gain and Diamond's gain because together we are the whole incarnate image of Christ on the earth.

Kingdom anthropologists operate from the fundamental belief that everyone belongs, that together we are a whole image, and that if someone's missing the picture is incomplete.

The kingdom of the world seeks to separate and systemize people groups by telling us to self-protect—move out of unsafe places, advance our own interests, gate our communities, protect our boundaries. But we see something altogether different in Jesus, who embodied and exemplified the will of heaven for earth. As Shane Claiborne writes:

> Everything in our society teaches us to move away from suffering, to move out of the neighborhoods where there is high crime, to move away from people who don't look like us. But

the gospel calls us to something altogether different. We are to laugh at fear, to lean into suffering, to open ourselves to the stranger. [This is the time] to remember how Jesus put on flesh and moved into the neighborhood. God getting born in a barn reminds us that God shows up in the most forsaken corners of the earth.[2]

We, the incarnation people, too rarely provide culture with Jesus' radically alternative style of living. Instead of doing what we've seen him doing—putting ourselves at risk, mingling with untouchables, becoming slaves to humanity—we duplicate a religious version of what the world is already achieving: keeping to our own kind.

Do you want to duplicate a system being perpetuated by the world?

Do you want to be a part of a system that continually pushes people out rather than inviting them in?

Nothing makes us closer imitators of Jesus than caring for our neighbors, no matter who they are or what they look like, no matter the strength of their odor or how high they might be that day.

I don't know where you are sitting or what you can see—a person or a plant or a piece of bread—but I invite you to look again and see the glory. The "holiness and the awful power and majesty of God" is present in the lowliest of people and the basest of places and the most ordinary of things and events. The alchemist is the anthropologist is the alchemist is the anthropologist, and we see the burning everywhere, even in a stable or on our knees in the grime of life or especially at the soup kitchen on Tuesday night.

In fact, woe unto us if we don't at least try to see it. Because the common teleports us to the Uncommon and back again, we rise and whirl and dance together in sky and sea and land.

This is the intention of a kingdom anthropologist: to represent the reality that there is nothing or nowhere or nobody too lowly or inauspicious that the presence of God can't be there too.

15

CRACK HOUSE FAMILY

The most fundamental premise a kingdom anthropologist holds is this: We are all connected. I'm connected to you and your mom's uncle and my husband and children and Diamond and Roger. We are all being held by the same structure, and we've all been breathing the same air since the beginning of time. It just keeps blowing around the globe, held close by gravity, and I often imagine that I've inhaled the same argon molecules that Jesus Christ exhaled ages ago. We are all a part of a universal energy field (read: Holy Spirit). We are even deeply intertwined with the natural world; the same breath that sustains us sustains the created order.

All life is precious because God spoke it into existence. Every single piece and particle are uniquely fashioned with the same matter and energy. The sea and the sky and the sand and the stars and the ash of us all filled with the elements of earthly and eternal, all kept pushing and thriving with the Spirit's divine vapor.

All things carry the DNA of deity and dust. But when I

open my eyes and look at the world around me, watch the news, listen to stories, read articles, view documentaries, and so on, I start to wonder if most of society lives under the basic assumption that we are all separate, that we are not connected at any level, let alone fundamentally. We've kept ourselves separated by cubicles and gated communities and fenced-in yards and dead-bolt doors. And I can't help but wonder: if we live under the basic assumption that we are all separate, then how will we ever come together like a fellowship of crossed-over anthropologists and care and connect and cultivate our love and peace and relationships to see kingdom come?

I'm going to step off a ledge here and even be so bold as to say that our ongoing and intentional disconnect is a real mental illness, one that's evolved from the systems we've created—systems of greed, success, status, power, economics, consumerism, and other agendas of self-interest. We've sold togetherness for a bowl of misconstrued stew because we thought we were hungry enough to sell our communal birthright.

How do we reverse this curse? What do we do to oppose the systems that tear us apart and leave people alone and cold and hungry on the streets? (Is lonely and cold and hungry on the streets the full potential of any human being? Step inside that skin for a minute.)

And how do we oppose the systems that destroy the elements of earth in the name of progress? (Is the destruction of the natural order being a good steward of the earth's full potential?)

Kingdom anthropologists ask these questions. The anthropologist alchemically sees that all people are intrinsically linked not just with one another, but with the entire created order, and seeks to generate a spirit of connection instead of division throughout the land. Maybe it's a small and slow revolution toward changing our own human hearts, learning to care on deeper levels, and we can't light all the fires. But if we could just start with ourselves and one small flame of change and then continue by passing the values and awareness down to our children, I have to believe that a love like this for humanity and the earth is possible and more than just a pipe dream.

Like a bushel full of barbarians, our boys came barreling in one day and they were sweating and panting and excitedly talking over each other because they had just witnessed another drug deal at the crack house across the street from us. The conversation went like this:

> **Boys:** Mama! Mama! Mama! We counted *three* drug
>   deals in fifteen *minutes*!
> **Me:** Oh, really? Papa and I saw two yesterday. I guess
>   you guys win. Hey, you didn't let anyone see you,
>   right? Cause as much as you bubs like to be all
>   Sherlock Holmesey and stuff, you're not ready for
>   the FBI, okay?
> **Boys:** We were hiding in our fort and using
>   binoculars. No one saw us!
> **Me:** All right. Just always be careful.

Wearing curiosity and camo like it's their only uniform, they shoo along to seek the next thrill in their day, and I go back to hulling my sinkful of pick-your-own strawberries. The languid motion and soothing rightness of preparing earth-fruit centers my city-dwelling self and propels my mind backward to my own growing-up days on that forty-acre farm in northern Michigan. And I'll be dad-gummed if my childhood story isn't a distant cry of different from the chapters we're writing with our kids right now. Dipping my hands below the water's surface for another strawberry feels like holiness and communion with Christ and a sacred prayer, and this is one of those sometimes that I ache for them to know what I knew back then—that life was as pure as the driven snow blowing off the shores of Lake Michigan and tasted like an endlessly reverent and wholesome pre-fall Eden feast.

When I was a little girl, coming into my skin and learning my own soul, I had fields and whole forests, what seemed like leagues of land to spin and skip and stretch and sprout on. My siblings and I gulped the country wind like it was nature's elixir and every lungful was free and we breathed it until we were consumed with aliveness. We were nature's own nymphs, lying flat on our backs in the acres of tall grasses, spread out like Xs next to the caroling crickets and singing cicadas, and I'm almost certain we reached straight up and hand-plucked stars right out of the untouched, indigo sky. We sifted our fledgling fingers through stalks of waist-high grain, raced our horses across rivers and through gravel pits, and played nighttime tag in the cornstalk rows. We built barns, milked goats, collected eggs, planted gardens, and we harvested hay from the pastures and honey from the bees we kept.

All this and so much more, and we couldn't stop our bodies from falling into bed every evening because we worked and played so hard. To say this kind of farm living was good would be a vast understatement. Creation was our cathedral, and we worshiped like tomorrow was going to be as utopian as yesterday and the next day and the next and the next.

In contrast to my own upbringing, the neighborhood in which we've chosen to sink our roots for the last twelve-plus years is an immensely messy place full of messy people who do messy things. On the surface, where we live now looks nice enough—with the Quinnipiac River flowing by us toward the ocean and the oyster boats harvesting from the river bottom and the historical homes sitting stately and seasoned with their vibrant hues and intricate trimmings. But most times the surface of a place is only skin-thin, and we know what really defines a place is what lies beneath the surface.

In general, our surroundings are loud and undignified, with hardness piercing in one side and shooting like fireworks out the other. Subwoofers blasting gritty rap music were the proverbial lullaby that rocked our babes to sleep, and they heard all the curse words—and I do mean all—before they were even potty trained. They've witnessed a peaceful family walk that turned into a desperate woman's pleading cry for rescue from injustice and the agony of seeing a young boy's abuse by the iron hand and viper voice of his grandmother.

Our house has been broken into three times; our bikes have been stolen and the copper pipes cut out of our basement plumbing lines. We get routinely woken up at punch-me-in-the-face-o'clock to the sound of drag racers screeching down the streets and police sirens screaming in pursuit. Several of our friends and neighbors have had their car tires stolen in the middle of the night, their vehicles left behind and propped up on cinder blocks.

There are prostitutes peddling their flesh on the worst corners and dealers selling drugs everywhere. A day doesn't go by that I don't see an exchange of goods. Our kids know what a "hand-off" and a "crack sack" look like, and they've seen and heard and asked about things that I didn't even know existed when I was their age.

The list goes on, and suffice it to say that we have seen some straight-up strange and stupid things around these parts. But where, if not in the middle of crooks and crazies, does the light need to shine?

Now, I don't know if you had a caution flag flip in your mind when you learned that we lived across from a crack house and our kids are observers in the middle of it, but I do know it's not entirely looked on with favor. I recently read a local person's opinion being offered on Facebook that children shouldn't be raised in our parts of New Haven because it's "ghetto . . . ghetto . . . ghetto . . . super ghetto . . . and unsafe." I sat back in my chair and had to think on that for a minute, and then the comeback that came to mind was nothing short of "really?" Because the gospel I hold in my bones believes that Jesus moved into this kind of neighborhood too. And maybe especially he came to the hard parts and the harsh people, and sometimes I'm not even exempt from this group. I mean, I'm not selling drugs or flesh, but I can be batty and broken in other ways—just ask my kids or my husband or my friends.

Here's the thing I would tell you now; why I'm so fierce about my "ghetto" land and her unsafe people: this place and the humanity within its limits have been a threshing floor where my character and composition were pulled apart and picked at and poked and prodded and thrown in the furnace to burn. And the fire blazed hot, and so many impurities turned to ash; this has been my refinement.

These people became my people when the callused hand of God—gently and firmly and without question or letting up—gripped the back of my neck and turned my head to point my eyes at all the mess. And that grip didn't release until I saw my neighbors and loved them just a small bit the way he does.

Are you feeling me and hearing me right now? He didn't let go until I saw my own messy reflection in their faces. He didn't let go until I adopted them into my heart and they, for better or for worse, became my family. Part of the divine plan was to make a kingdom anthropologist out of me, and this ghetto was where he got the job done. The kingdom anthropologist in me has been born from living next door to the nincompoops and nutjobs and quacks and mongrels and misfits. I would put quotation marks around all those words, but I think you know that these "low and despised in the world" (1 Corinthians 1:28 ESV) are men and women who bear the body of Jesus around on their shaky, shifty legs.

They are mine and I am theirs, regardless of if they want me to be. And what they don't know is that I walk the alleys and avenues all over and around them, praying my every exhale out and leaving Spirit floating like fractals of smoke in my wake. I walk the alleys and avenues just so I can usher healing into the land and so I can look every person right in the eyes and beam my love and exuberant greetings, hoping that something of the Jesus Christ in me will get caught in their hearts and something of the Jesus in them will get caught in mine, glory be and kingdom come.

There's this one wee little man who smells like an ashtray full of cigarette butts and stale cologne on top of that and unwashed skin to boot. I see him every morning when I'm out taking my daily constitutional across both bridges and around the river, and he resolutely keeps his head bent toward the ground and has never once looked me in the face, no matter how much I will him to. He will not lift his soul-windows for anything, but I'm always ready with my smile just in case. And yesterday when he walked by me again and didn't raise his head an inch, I wept because I still don't know what color his eyes are . . . and he's my brother.

✱

We know, of course we know—it isn't the safest area to raise our kids. But for us, what's more important than playing life safe is living life rooted where we sense we're commissioned as a family. In the midst of all the crazies and colorfuls, we're teaching our crazy and colorful sons how to grow their hearts for humanity and how to extend grace toward the rougher aspects of existence. We are whispering to their spirits about story and nurturing their ability to really see the people who get pushed to the margins. Margins are where the misfits go, but it's not the Bible that tells me so.

So we choose to mix our molecules with this strange and tired place, and we invite our boys to look for a deeper, bigger story. We want them to know that we're no better and just as human as the guys and gals next door.

And just in case you forget, look again, my sons, and you will see your own reflection coming back to you. Look again, my sons, and you will see Jesus.[1]

The kingdom anthropologist always sees Jesus.

Together we're discovering how to love and ache for the downtrodden, how to pray for their wounds and extend compassion because maybe some people have never known that life could be beautiful or kind or that God had any goodwill toward them. Maybe all they've ever had for breakfast was dust or drugs or despair, and they can't imagine a way out of their own hellhole.

Our boys are learning how to keep their eyes and edges soft and tender toward human beings, and already they would tell you that each and every one of our neighbors are the brothers and sisters of their souls—family—even the dealers across the street and the prostitutes on the corner. We're guiding them around the margins and inspiring them to love and stretch their worldview and boundaries. And by the time they're adults? By then I can only imagine and hope that they'll have canyons of compassion carved inside their guts.

So maybe we shouldn't be raising our kids here as some people say. But here is where we are passing down one of our own family traditions of teaching our kids to swirl the stuff of heaven with the stuff of earth around us, awakening our kids to the reality that they are alchemists and anthropologists in a place full of people who need to be seen, for the same reasons we need to be seen too.

We're doing our darndest to grow our kids in the "ghetto" where we've been planted. And country, city, or suburbs—one is not better or more right than the other. Maybe we won't live exactly here forever, but we do all need to live in reference to one another's experiences and stories in order to create a more holistic understanding of our global family and more effectively transmit the "God is love" we Christians keep talking about.

Do you sense a longing to bring an anthropological economy to your neighborhood that mirrors the walks and ways of Jesus when he moved from place to place, seeing people and preaching a new kingdom order? Wherever you live and whoever your neighbor is, kingdom anthropologists, let us come together and see everyone like we've lived inside their skin and everything else for its full potential—the singular reason being we are commissioned to be Christ shadows, to walk right in his wake and move our limbs in rhythm with what we've seen him do.

The apostle Paul tells us in Ephesians that a Christian is, by definition, someone who mimics God: "Watch what God does, and then you do it" (5:1). In other words and because repetition helps me remember: a Christian, in its original proposition, is one who follows and looks like Christ—nothing more and nothing less. When his kingdom is manifested through us, it doesn't look like a building or a program or a group. It looks like the not-cautious, extravagant love Jesus had and has for everything and everyone. It looks like living in our neighborhoods in such a way that invites compassion and inclusivity and intentional living without letting common assumptions keep us from seeing our streets and suburbs and society for their full potential.

16

CROSS-DRESSERS AND KUMBAYAS

*T*he kingdom of God looks like Jesus, and Jesus looks like the places he shouldn't go and the stories he shouldn't tell and the miracles he shouldn't perform on the Sabbath and the people he shouldn't associate with or touch and the enemies he shouldn't forgive as he's strung up and dying against the splinters of a cross.

The actual embodiment of God's kingdom was a walking house of taboos, an atmosphere of no-nos, a renegade to contemporary culture.

Crazy vanguardist he—and the greatest kingdom anthropologist who ever lived because he didn't let human labels ("unclean!" "living in sin!" "tax collector!") mask his ability to see everyone with a love and compassion that evidenced he'd been inside their skin. He never let the labels keep him from seeing everything else under the sun for its full potential.

Jesus wrote his own rules of engagement and those rules all boiled down to one: God = Love.

We, the followers, can only yearn and sometimes beg for a

love that big and bold and beautiful to take our hearts hostage. We can only go low as often as possible and ask without ceasing for the Biographer of love to school us in his ways.

"Teach me how to love."

"Teach me how to love."

"Teach me how to love."

Over and over and over may we plead with a fist against our chests and a consuming heat for the hope of being micro-mirrors of his macro-majesty. Kingdom come.

The loving will open our eyes and train us to see Jesus everywhere. To see how he penetrates every particle of the world through and through. He can be found anywhere—in a human face, in a speck of hallowed dust viewed under a microscope.

What a wealth of riches he offers when he says "Follow me."

I want to follow Jesus because I have an insatiable ache and affection for him. I am haunted day and night—in my waking, sleeping, doing, being—by the most riveting figure in the history of everything. I *love* Jesus.

And just because the One I love was here where my body is now bound, just because he walked on this earth I inhabit, there is no terrain anywhere on this whole orbiting green and blue ball that isn't holy. Because he wove them in the darkness and wetness of his mother's womb, there is no person anywhere who isn't worthy.

Do you believe it?

This is enough to remind us to fall into our days holding the truth that we are standing on sanctified ground and every bush and tree is swaying with God's breath, and every scoundrel and saint is known to him by name and nature and numbered hairs—the beautiful and the base, the kids and the criminals. All of them.

Look beneath the surface of the rose garden and your daily bread and behind the back of your enemy and see. He's there.

Kingdom anthropologists, come. People of the sight, come. Come to the least likely places and where you're needed most or seemingly not needed at all and alchemically reveal to the watching world the actual face of the living God.

Speak the prayers: "Teach me how to love today and how to see today and how to hold the world and humanity to my breast today—because I saw you embrace them first, and I'm so passionately determined to go where you go and do what I see you doing."

Let us speak the prayers and make the "further up and further in" journey that will allow us to sense and detect his animated presence everywhere, even when it seems to be nowhere.

Kingdom anthropologists, come.

There's something otherworldly about the Loaves and Fishes food pantry in downtown New Haven, where the disadvantaged go on Saturday mornings to get their brown bags filled with free food. Our not-disadvantaged family goes too, and we're dressed differently (nicely) and we smell clean; we look like "the helpers." Even here where everyone is blending—volunteers and vagrants—the status lines are drawn. If you're careless you can remain separate even when everyone's together.

This is a place where a certain type of people go because for whatever reason or life story they don't have enough. Mainstream society has labeled this group as "the marginalized" because they live in the margins—in the one inch of space on the left side of lined paper, on the outside of where "regular" folk make their beds. But here's the thing: Jesus turned everything backward when he established his crossed-over, alternate-reality kingdom, which leads me to believe that the margins where all these irregulars live are actually the real, wide-open palaces, and the toothless vagabonds, crazy misfits, and destitute bums are the real royalty. Do you believe it?

As a family we've chosen this space and these people because everyone can come as they are and everyone is accepted unconditionally, even though most are some level of screwball—scraggly and unkempt and bent under the yoke of survival—and nobody cares where you've come from or where you're going.

We are at home in this basement place where hungry people come for bread because we are hungry for Bread too. The ache in our bellies for all kinds of sustenance binds us together, and there is never a greater sense of belonging than in this space where our souls and bones and toes are catapulted to the center of an unwashed, undignified cacophony of quirky and preposterous people.

I love—love, I tell you—the loudmouths and the maniacs and the sea of skin colors and wrinkle patterns. I love the offending scents, bad language, and indecent behavior. I love the spectrum and volume of energy buzzing in the atmosphere and knocking from drywalls, the graceless chaos of pushing and shoving and crashing. I even loved it when someone started spit-screaming at me because I couldn't understand the name he mumbled at the registration table.

But I especially love the reluctant acceptance here, the show of community. Somehow we all know we're chained into one another's lives, stale dreams and broken seams and all. Our individual ships are sinking, but together we manage to stay afloat one more day.

This wild scene of sanctified savagery feels like church to me. And I'm able to find a refuge when we show up and choose to look for all the ways Jesus breaks out of me and my family and everyone else too, splits our earthen vessels right open as if to say, "We're together and here I am too. Let's get this party started."

Do you want to know why I see so much sacred glory in this place, in the fruitcakes and psychopaths, the unwashed flesh and clogged toilets, the ever-present profanity? I'll give you three guesses, but the first two don't count, and his name is Jesus.

I see Jesus everywhere, and being his follower means that one of my main objectives is to see him wherever, whenever, however I'm conceivably able because this is our foretaste of heaven. Seeing and being with Jesus is what makes us feel less like exiles living in a bizarre land.

But can't I see Jesus somewhere nicer? Why not in the sunrise or mountaintop, in a pristine cathedral or an art museum? Why not seek him in a newborn's face or reflected in the gaze of a lover?

Well, yes. Of course we can see him there. And I confess to wishing sometimes that I could just stay where it's clean and safe, where there's nothing untoward or annoying confronting my scope or sphere of relationship.

But our overarching family value is Jesus' very own "follow me," and that value doesn't allow us to play it preserved and unthreatened. That value decides our fate, and our fate is in his footsteps, for better or for worse.

More often than not, our fate leads us to the strangest places, seeing the Stranger in the strangest people.

There was a Saturday morning in particular when we went to the food pantry and I immediately sensed the hypnosis of heaven drifting among the rafters and walls and concrete under my Converse shoes. It felt like Christmas morning around a warm fire or coming home to the arms of family—a place so familiar and heady I could've smelled it from my sleep.

The sights and sounds were cascading with the quality of a dream, and the air moved like gauze, even though the actual scene was a bona fide jungle of battered humanity. And I stood in the midst of it all and found myself acutely aware I was one of them—chief of all the riffraff creatures—even though you wouldn't know it to look at me.

You can't always see my ego, the toxic trap of my messy mind or the other silent and deadly ways in which I manifest my scruffy humanity—not the way you can see a torn T-shirt or a missing tooth—but I wear them nevertheless. Our scars didn't match, but the fact that we've all got them in varying ways connects us even deeper, binds us together.

On that anthropological, alchemic morning I was feeling even more connected than usual. By the time I'd registered the seventieth food-pantry patron, a transvestite man with an outrageous ensemble of Goodwill-gathered patterns and styles, complete with gilded hoop earrings and bright ruby-red lipstick, flaunted in like a red-carpet diva or a runway model during New York Fashion Week. Within minutes he started serenading the crowd.

And here's the thing: he was singing hymns.

All morning long, around and around and around, he braided himself slowly through all the food-seeking bodies with an open hymnbook in his hands, singing hosanna song after hosanna song. The whole scene was golden and glorious and enough to make a grown man weep if he was paying any kind of attention to Who was actually happening in that place.

Our cross-dressing singer was so beautiful, with his hymnal spread wide and his booming voice busting through our hearts. It doesn't get more vibrant or variegated than that, and in my estimation this cross-dressing, hosanna-singing man represented the Glue that stuck all us kids together that day. Not only did the colorful complexity of his character invite everyone else to come just as they were—with all the strangeness and skeletons they stood up under—but also because the first song he belted out was none other than "Kumbaya," the tune originally correlated with human and spiritual unity, closeness and compassion.

He was a peculiar prophet in our midst, and his chanting of the hallelujah songs was an "Our Father who art in heaven, hallowed be thy name" kind of prayer that set the table for all of us, an invitation for all of us to come together, sit down, and eat.

I paused. I breathed. I shut my eyes for only a moment, grateful to see Jesus once more in this likely place for him to be. And you must know that part of the reason I place myself in these spaces is just because I want to be close to the One my soul longs for, to touch a square of his garment or pull him in for a full-frontal hug. I want to be near enough to feel his face under my fingers, the warm planes of his cheekbones. Know his stripes and scent and Spirit.

The whole eccentric event was made for dancing and hollering, and I was grinning as wide as the lousy limitations of my face would allow. The feeling was something you might have when a brief period of time becomes shamelessly pure and indescribably right and incandescently beautiful. I was practically bursting.

And all the craziness and "Kumbaya" singing doesn't stop me from pausing within the bedlam just to pull the essence of my Jesus in and down to my solar plexus. He was there and the movement and motion of the "Kumbaya" singer mimicked the fluid presence of Jesus in the room. He was weaving and blending his form around and through the earthbound bodies in that ethereal, gossamer way of his—touching shoulders, bathing feet, and bending close to hold and deliver a widespread smile to everyone. He was knitting us close and whole—one body, one family.

There are no words for what it feels like to know him as someone touchable on this side of the grave.

Of all the reasons for dragging my rear end out of bed on a Saturday morning, it doesn't get better or brighter than the day God chose a cross-dresser of the world to reveal his Son.

✱

Fyodor Dostoyevsky writes in *The Brothers Karamazov*:

> Love [people] even in [their] sin, for that is the semblance of Divine Love and is the highest love on earth. Love all God's creation, the whole and every grain of sand of it. Love every leaf, every ray of God's light. Love the animals, love the plants, love everything. If you love everything, you will perceive the divine mystery in things. Once you perceive it, you will begin to comprehend it better every day. And you will come at last to love the whole world with an all-embracing love.[1]

The kingdom of Christ was designed to be recognizable from the kingdom of the world by its most distinguishing trait—fundamental, nonjudgmental, unconditional love. Kingdom anthropologists lasso this kind of love, nurture this kind of love, give away this kind of love, and they invite others to the absolute, transformative power of this all-embracing love. Everyone and everything is tenderly held and healed inside its redemptive quality.

Christ's "love was not cautious but extravagant" (Ephesians 5:2), so do not be a miser with what you've been given or get distracted from the sole purpose of shadowing his steps. Jesus is here now, and the kingdom anthropologist goes out to find him in the low and the despised, employing bags of handed-out groceries, stale donuts, and cheap coffee in his service. His Spirit floats between, drifts and cascades and fills up everything, from pieces of food to evergreen forests to pounds of flesh. He is to be found everywhere and anywhere—above and between and below.

Are you having trouble seeing Jesus? Maybe you just need to look a little longer with the eyes of your soul (which were fashioned for alchemy) and feel a little deeper with your blood-pumping heart (which was fashioned for anthropology). And practice—if you want to be a kingdom anthropologist, you need to make a regular practice of looking at people and the world through Jesus' eyes and engaging them as Jesus would.

Put a date on the calendar, go find church in the wild, and look for the face of Jesus in any and every character you come across. If there are particular areas or certain types of people in the created order that you have difficulty loving, then fall hard on your knees and remember the only prayer you should pray: "Teach me how to love." Examine the assumptions you might ascribe to or the human systems you might have bought stock in that don't allow all-embracing love to flow through you. And ask the Holy Ghost to help you get free for love's sake.

All we've got is one another and this one awesome kingdom to point to. So go the extra mile, do the hard work, turn your cheek a million times, and love your enemies like it's your job.

Because it is.

Art

17

REDEFINING ART (LIFE AS ART)

I t's most likely that we've never met, that I don't know who you are or the specifics of your story, what your vices look like or how many victories you've celebrated or the number of scars you count on your arm or soul at night before your head hits the pillow. Have you been to hell and back, or has your life been smooth-sea sailing—or has it been some combination of the two?

I might wonder if your chromosomes are more Y and less X or the other way around, if you're a youngin' or all grown up. I might wonder about the shade of your skin, the hue of your hair, the intensity of your irises, the stretch of your smile, if you're stout or slim or strong, solo or hitched. I might wonder at your hobbies or occupations, interests or talents, the places and people that get your all-out energy.

I don't have the answers to my questions, which is to say that your intimate details leave me hanging with their unknowns, but I so desire that a small anything within the letters of these pages has meant something to you because I went inside the bowels of my being with a backhoe and excavated the best pieces of what I know to be true. And here's the part where I'm hoping everything I've offered in this book gets secured together—the part where we harness our avant-garde approach (unorthodox, experimental, nonconformist) and weld it to the agents of alchemy (the stuff of heaven) and anthropology (the stuff of earth) and go create some rarefied and wonderful and only-you kind of art.

This whole book has been my art expressed and held up to the sky in a poured-out attempt to fill in my spot up there. It is my soul on display outside my body—I have never felt more exposed. And you probably noticed already that I didn't wait until the "art section" to reveal art. Every story told in every chapter written was and is pulsing and blooming with the ways in which I offer my life as art.

Making a fine art out of living is who I am and what I do. I consider myself a life artist, and my media are everywhere. I listen on high alert and watch with a wideness to my vision and a spreading of my soul; then I get busy weaving and painting and fusing and transmuting my lowly little bits of atoms and atmosphere, tools and towns and tears, survivors and stars and shovels. I create rhythms and rituals and stories and moments of beautiful, brazen, wholehearted art.

Making a fine art out of living is what we're all invited and purposed and commissioned to do, each in our different ways.

And when all of us are joined together offering a lifestyle of kingdom art, we can boldly break through the synthetic systems we've built and perpetuated and light the universe on fire with a great, enormous love. We can color the cosmos with a united sign that points toward the absolute grandeur of God.

Do you believe it?

I've read a lot of interpretations and opinions and thoughts and descriptions and commentaries about art—especially in preparation for writing on this theme—but the definition that kept coming to the top, the one that I felt held the most depth to me, came from the innermost interior of my own marrow.

Here it is: art is your soul outside your body.

Stop and think about that for a minute.

Art is your soul outside your body; it's the thousands and thousands of ways that you choose to reveal yourself to the world—you and nobody else made manifest. It's the way you make your coffee and the specific sound of your free laugh and what you create with your own ten fingers and your getting-ready routine as well as the pictures you paint (if you paint them), the music you make (if you make it), and any number of other endeavors more commonly thought of as artistic.

This stripped-down definition of art is not said to minimize the work of fine artists, but rather to invite and include anyone outside that category to reimagine the vast rolling hills of creative energy already embedded in their precious makeup, flowing through their singular genetic code and to reconnect—if necessary—with the birthright of their own artistic nature.

Art is not only something made by a subculture of exceptionally gifted and accredited individuals; *art is a divine birthright gifted to each individual.*

Art is everything you do with your soul outside your body, and it cannot be taken from you, undone or divested. *But you can fail to realize it.*

You can fail to be awakened to the truth of your *only* parts. You can squash or stomp your essence to death by allowing the voices of mass culture or the lies of an enemy to suffocate it with the errant sounds of untruth.

Your art matters, which is just another way to say: *your soul matters.*

Your soul matters, your art matters, and did you know that everything you do and how you do it—your art—is so visible it's like you're wearing it tattooed on your sleeve? It's truly a vulnerable reality to have when art is simply the stuff of you—the manifestation of your specifics dictated by your resources—out and about, promenading in front of the watching world.

But as with all three of the other themes, I want to be sure to place the meaning of art in my open palms and hold it humbly and tenderly while we walk to the cross, bow it down on the ground like an offering, then pick it up again and carry it to the other side.

What is different about art on the other side of Jesus?

The main difference is that it's not just about ourselves.

On the other side of Jesus our interlocking circle of art is a whole woven contribution that reflects the divine.

Whether what you create is a painting on canvas or a drawing on paper or a pattern to sew or the unique ways you ensemble your clothes or craft your family rhythm or your style of living or the values you maintain—it's about you, yes, but it's more about the collective work being held up against the great big open atmosphere, beaming the image of Christ into a burned-out and bloodshot world.

On the other side of Jesus, art is an offering, a death to self that births new life, a gift, a contribution to the greater whole. You are made to create and give it away and create and give it away and create and give it away. So take your molecules and your moments and your unprecedented mess and the intoxicated music of your life and make a masterpiece that reflects the truth.

Because on the other side of Jesus, art is a revelation of the kingdom, a kingdom revealing God through billions of different kaleidoscopic expressions. Art, your art, is absolutely vital because your art is how Jesus is made known to the world.

And this is the part where I ask you to look into my eyes so you know and hear what it's like for me to speak a fact over you. Imagine I'm reaching through states and cities, counties and countries, and I'm grabbing your hand and pulling you in and everything you've heard to the contrary of what I'm about to say is a lie.

Are you listening with both your ears and the receptors in your skin and brain and belly?

Your art is vital because it shoots a specific—as in never-again-repeated—beacon of light into the sky, making kingdom come on earth. And when all our beacons are shining together, the whole is revealed.

You have to go all avant-garde with the elements between your fingers and your creative self engaged because if you're only creating what you have already seen done, then your unique shimmer and swelling color is absent from the celestial sphere and a you-sized shape will leave a hole in the cosmos.

Your uniquely avant-garde art is a declaration of the Almighty—maybe just a tiny corner of his elbow or ear or chin or skin, but that tiny corner will set you and the captives and the kingdom free.

I will ask for the umpteenth time in this book: Do you believe it?

Everything is made from the breath of God and the dust of stars, and it's the creativity of God that arranges stardust into stalks of wheat and bowls of grapefruit and herds of wild mustangs and humankind. Divine-made resources must be adored. And through reverent adoration, we—the artists—who have been made in the image of this great Artist, hold the work made of his hands—the abundance of his resources—and manifest forward by creating creation further. So stalks of wheat become loaves of bread and bales of hay. Grapefruit becomes juice and breakfast and still life paintings. Mustangs run graceful and free across the plains. And men and women and children copy the Creator by making beauty any way we can, even by the way we lead our ordinary lives.

The great Artist made artists who make art that reflects back to the great Artist.

Once we combine our avant-garde intentions with alchemy— the stuff of heaven—and anthropology—the stuff of earth—we manifest our souls outside our bodies in ways that go far beyond what history and society have classified as art. And our creative expressions are offered as gifts back to the kingdom, reflecting God in the unique ways that each of us alone can do.

For example, art can happen when it's raining grey drops outside, peppering the black asphalt and earth-dirt with heaven's impartial, christening water. Even inside the house it smells like truth, damp and heavy and pure like creation's church, and my imagination is pressed close to cold panes of windowed glass. I can almost feel the taste of liquid silver on my tongue, and this absurd little human heart inside a chest of flesh flips over and—oh, dear God—the sound of the rain on the roof.

The wet drumming above has me in wave after wave of rapture and turns my soul schoolgirl-giddy, and I'm sure if my spirit were to expand out any further or rise up any higher, it would be away and gone from its home in and around my body. There is the fog descending to offer his filmy, floating mist to the dewy dimension of autumn's stormy canvas.

Under the wet and the grey there are Infinite-illustrated leaves dancing their colors in a lover's waltz with the subliminal brush of a wandering-by-with-a-whistle kind of breeze. They know it is their highest praise just to be, and I am noticing; my eyes are eating elements and landscape and the participants like soul food. It is my own high worship, the watchfulness and the mindfulness and the listening. The whole collection seems to speak to me: "Welcome to the real world, daughter of Eve and ether. Open your God-given gifts and join the great cathedral."

Art can happen with nothing more than a moment of wake-fulness and whatever is in front of you—a window pane, a pile of leaves, some wet weather.

Or soft lamplight and a kitchen table.

The kitchen clocks turns 10:32 p.m., and we've scrubbed our teeth clean and checked on the kids and turned off all the lights but one. It's early to sleep for my husband and me, the usual midnighters. But in the midst of this going-to-bed routine, something about the soft glow of the last-on forty-watt bulb, something about how the kitchen air suspended so quiet and crowded with a full measure of importance, something about the simmering of my insides hooked my attention to high alert and slow-motioned my spirit to stillness.

I knew I was being seduced by Someone to go deep into this seemingly regular and very ordinary moment, and words were invoked from my heart as I turned unhurried to my husband.

"Hey, hon, do you know what we've never done before?"

He angles his head out the bathroom door and says, "What?" with a smile, his pointer finger sliding the contact lens from one of his dark-brown eyes.

"We've never sat at this kitchen table at exactly this time of night with just this light on." My lips arc at the corners, soliciting him with a silent invitation. This spouse of mine understands me well and knows that I want to make a memory, make some magical art out of what seems like thin-air nothing.

So we begin by curving our tired and collapsing carcasses into the kitchen-table chairs and inviting our own perceptions to shift and embrace and stay there in a mysterious time warp of uncharted minutes as we allow the mystic to unfurl around our skin. She whispers her presence in the space between us, and never has our life-sharing or soul-connecting been better than that hour of unexpected, unplanned intertwining.

Art can happen without any traditional supplies at all. Even when you and your spouse are sleepy, when no one else is there to witness what's being made, the moment can still be a signpost that points to and praises the divine.

Art is your soul outside your body, and there are so many ways to manifest where your uniqueness meets up with God's gifts. Look for ways to unconventionally and untraditionally engineer beauty or a minute into something more. Ripple the fabric of your home, your city, the universe. Use what you can touch—steel rings and cucumbers and flower petals and a photograph from fifty years ago—and combine it with what you can't contain—ocean mist and ultraviolet rays and whipping wind and elephant-shaped clouds or just the pattern and flow of your day. Take your imagination seriously and rediscover the wonder of making a molecule or a mountain's worth of art. Get lost in the gentle movement and overwhelming sensation of making something higher and bigger than yourself, something that connects us all together and gives us a sense of place in exile.

Something that gives us all a foretaste of heaven.

One of the most foundational requirements for being a good artist is the ability to be quiet and to pay attention. Frederick Buechner urges:

> Listen to your life. See it for the fathomless mystery that it is. In the boredom and pain of it no less than in the excitement and gladness: touch, taste, smell your way to the holy and hidden heart of it because in the last analysis all moments are key moments, and life itself is grace.[1]
>
> You are alive. It needn't have been so. It wasn't so once and it will not be so forever. But it is so now. . . . Take any day and be alive in it. The world is to open.[2]

Being alive in a day that might not have been, as a person who might not have been, is what it means to be an artist. If you are fully alive—that is, more than just breathing and going through the motions—then you are ready, willing, and able to create. Find a new way to do the same old thing, change your rhythm just a bit to better reflect who you are, and stand in the same spot long enough to see it differently.

You were carefully crafted to be an intimate witness and a thoughtful, prayerful composer, orchestrating every moment of living that you humanly can into stories and paintings and choruses of unspeakable depth. Your media are the stuff of heaven in the air around you and the stuff of the active, dynamic, synergistic, God-breathed earth—raw materials you are invited to combine and craft into fine art. Your tools are alchemy and anthropology and your unique avant-garde point of view. Your fingerprints can brush against a velvet curtain hanging between the seen and unseen spaces and make visible that which the world cannot perceive with their naked eyes.

Be the art. Watch how your soul lives outside your body. If it isn't authentically reflecting the particulars of who you are with holy breath inside you, then revisit the floor with your prostrate body and ask to see the naked truth of yourself.

18

MARRIAGE AS ART

Why marriage?

This is the question that came to me on the eve of our tenth anniversary, an anniversary Austin and I were celebrating with a vow-renewal ceremony. We had chosen to have the ceremony because we'd been down some hard roads during that decade and aimed to mark the redemption of our story with witnesses, wet cheeks, new oaths, and popped bottles. Even so, the question haunted me: *Why is marriage so important to who we are and what we say we believe in?* I inquired again and again and for the hope of grasping and chaining ourselves to an answer that every other answer could find its roots in when the day was done and the deeds happened dark.

Have you ever found yourself in a similar marriage situation, where you appeal for answers that don't come skimmed off the top, where the surface responses aren't enough to anchor you to an eternal commitment?

Marriage is not quite the starry-eyed experience we might

imagine when we're standing at the altar dressed in white and naivete. And marriage is so much more than a product of the conventional reasons we might figure we're getting tied together for.

Marriage is a terrifyingly complex, vibrant, and vital organism—mysterious, powerful, paradoxically delicate. Symbolically it contains one of the deepest mysteries of the universe, so fathomless I'm certain we don't have the brainpower to ring our understanding around it. And the best and abiding way I have found to treat such a rare and fragile gift is to view the pure expression of it as an extraordinary art form, so singular and synergistic that no one between the ether and the deep blue sea will manifest the ebb and flow and go and come again just the way me and mine—and you and yours—do.

The journey to discovering Austin and my own unique approach to marriage-as-art began with the comeback to my "why marriage?" question, a comeback that hooked me and took me where I didn't expect to go—and how would you like to crash a wedding in Cana with me?

The Wind is pulsing in currents, vibrations, drafting in and out and gently swooping around the guests and their glamour, wafting with the mingled perfume of flesh and food, the music of laughter and tears, and the buzzing of an earth gone drunk on its own anticipation. He's sitting at the table—a strange and somewhat serious guest—watching the to and fro of everything; his eyes don't miss a posture, a gesture, a beat, a cadence, or even an atom or piece of dust as it rises from the land like it's alive.

He is inside himself and above himself, watching from within and from without. The world is his pearl and his cross to wear over his bent back when the time comes for getting nailed up. Love marks his face with lines and wrinkles and joy, too, for what is set before him. But now he sets aside his somewhat seriousness and parties like the rest and best of them. He's inhaling wine and exhaling sacramental symbolism into the air; his breath impregnates the atmosphere with microscopic droplets of purpose and mystery. Something is about to get born here, even though his time has not yet come.

Mostly what he can think about in the midst of the revelry is his own birth and the one big reason why he got born all this way into a dystopian world, contracted and contracted and contracted and gutturally heaved headlong into the hay, cast into our shadowy space so he could grow up, put a ring on it, and marry himself to the whole globe with a straight-up baffling, messy, and downright incessant love. His entire intents and purposes as a Groom coming to love his bride are being acted out on the small stage of this Cana wedding, and he's lost in a waking dream of intimate mystery—rings and promises, held hands and sealed kisses, banquets and one-day sacrifice.

The Wind is burgeoning now, blooming past stone walls and reaching with delicate, fanciful wreaths of invisible God-fingers, soaking the scene with the deeper meanings that are meant to be inside every wedding ritual. This is so one day we can look back on an ancient story and spend days and days until eternity wondering what was really going on at that site of Jesus' first miracle.

"The story of the wedding at Cana has a curious luminousness about it," writes Frederick Buechner about that long-ago party, "the quality almost of a dream where every gesture, every detail, suggests the presence of meaning beneath meaning, where people move with a kind of ritual stateliness, faces melting into other faces, voices speaking words of elusive but inexhaustible significance."[1]

Can you imagine being there and sensing what all this feels and smells like and how it explodes your soul and rises in your chest? His reverie is deep, his flesh is warm, energy transmits from his skin. People are staring in his face and losing themselves forever in the ancient pools of his young eyes.

His mama breaks into the scene because she just overheard the servants talking about a beverage deficiency, and she petitions her son for help because the party planner, of all things, failed to order enough wine. He tells his mama something about his time not yet having arrived and don't put the cart before the donkey. But mamas are discerning, and Mary is no exception. She tells the servants to do whatever her son says.

Before he can issue any orders, he hears a familiar whisper and the sense of it comes through the surface of his naked arm. The Father speaks to the Son: "I've arranged a marriage for you. It's time."

Without any added ado, he tells the servants to brim thirty clay jars with water and slip in their dippers and fill the host's cup. "The best for last!" the host exclaims, and the miracle that takes place is heard around the whole thirsty world. Creation hadn't known it was holding its breath until just now. Never again will refreshment be in short supply. Living water has finally come.

And with this single phenomenon the bride was birthed. The Groom set out from Cana anticipating his own wedding after what he knew would be a three-year-long wooing—feral and foolish, fraught with gravel and glory.

Then, with dust and grime in all the fissures of his rugged feet, he stumped and lumbered along a far and rocky trail to the top of Death Hill because that's where his chapel was and he was going to get married. Vows had never looked so bloody before, with the words "I do" written with red ribbons of split-wide sacrifice.

He is cross-eyed now, and his mouth tastes like spit with grit and shards of metal, but not one of his brides will ever need to wonder if he was serious in love or not. So he damns himself until Sunday by saying, "I take you . . . to have and to hold . . . from this day forward, in sickness and in health, in riches and in poverty . . . as long as we both shall live"—which, in his case, is nothing short of a never-ending forever.

Right after Austin and I were pronounced man and wife, our friend and officiator, Jim, voiced these words over us: "You, Austin, and you, Erika—together—represent the image of Christ."

The image of Christ.

If what our friend said is true and we choose to believe it, if we desire to model our lives after who Jesus was and what Jesus gave, then Austin and I don't get to decide which parts of him to take or leave. We are all-or-nothing kind of people, and we resolved on *all* a long time ago. Which means the image I just parsed and particularized—we represent that too. We represent the image of a Christ who gave himself utterly to the whole world, got busted like an eggshell in the process, garbled out a "please forgive them" after he'd been carved like a lamb on a butcher block and beaten to a street-accident pulp, couldn't lift up his own hung head, and perished at the end of it all.

We—our marriage—includes the representation of that broken Christ.

But we didn't really understand that then. Neither of us knew we were saying yes to the breadth and depth of that gruesome image. We thought marriage was a happily-ever-after with the top down and the wind in our hair, not a bleeding sideshow or some brutal route where our guts would get spilled.

But our guts did get spilled shortly after this one man named Peter bent his six-foot-six frame over our married feet and prophesied with verve in his vocals and intensity in his closed-tight eyes that thousands and thousands would gather in great sweeping circles and sit around our married love, gleaning edible and nourishing fruits from the prepared feast Austin and I shared. We didn't have much time to reflect on the fine points or possibilities of Peter's prophetic vision, because less than a month later our love collapsed and fell against the bottom floor of our supposedly rock-solid foundation, shattering into a million little shard-sharp pieces.

To say we didn't see it coming is the abyss of understatements. Before all the breaking, in fact, we both reflected to our good friends that we were "the happiest we've ever been."

What a bunch of bull malarkey that turned out to be. Or maybe not so much malarkey as cluelessness; we honestly didn't know we were uttering a dishonest statement. Come to find out, we didn't know ourselves very well at all. Both Austin and I had shoved down and bottled up storm after storm after storm, all of which were merging and evolving into a tornado twisting in our torsos. But we were blithely oblivious to the mounting pressure until an event took place that absolutely and unequivocally yanked the rug from under our feet and loosed the inside cyclone.

Our faces greeted the hard and barbed ground when the wind howled, and we woke up all the way to lucidity. But lucidity turned out to be the scariest place of all because I was not who I thought I was and neither was my husband, and for the love of all things holy, could anything be salvaged from the wreckage of this bleak and brutal existence?

Austin and I fell into wedded nonbliss almost overnight, and our married eyes still look back and marvel that we decided—nothing less than a sheer-grit decision—that in spite of our stupid choices and our sullied circumstances, neither of us was going anywhere. And by "going" I mean hit the highway running and don't look back because the house we built in the sand was sinking, and the promises we'd thought were for better or for worse had turned out shockingly flimsy before the rigors of reality.

About the time Austin and I were gritting our still-married teeth and deciding to stay together "in spite of," I read a beautiful little book by Madeleine L'Engle. *Walking on Water* is about the intersection of faith and art, and it's full of intimate, attentive, and reverent observations. What I found in this work of syllabary and soul proved to be a treasure worth mining, especially some specific words in her last chapter that hammered like truth flattening down my door:

> Art is an affirmation of life, a rebuttal of death.
>
> And here we blunder into paradox again, for during the creation of any art form, art which affirms the value and the holiness of life, the artist must die.
>
> To serve a work of art, great or small, is to die, to die to self.
>
> If the artist is to be able to listen to the work, he must get out of the way; or, more correctly, since getting out of the way is not a do-it-yourself activity, he must be willing to be got out of the way, to be killed to self . . . in order to become a servant of the work.
>
> To serve a work of art is almost identical with adoring the Master of the Universe. . . . not to find self, but to lose self in order to be found.[2]

I know this quote is about traditional forms of art, but do you see what I see? Do you see how it can apply to marriage art as well? Do you see how following and repeating the pattern of death to self that Jesus set forth leads to the resurrected offerings of our best work, including marriage?

I saw it back then, and Austin saw it when I shared the book with him, and seeing it worked in us like pain and hope. If our marriage was to affirm and value the holiness of life, affirm and value and reflect the holiness of God's love for the world, then both of us needed to walk the Calvary path to our own destruction. We both needed to die in different (and cyclical) ways before the artwork of our marriage could symbolically be lifted up.

So there we stood all flummoxed and flabbergasted at what had happened to us and what we had made happen. But on the other side of this and that and the other thing, our union was no longer the untried, untested, untaught union of our youth. Rather it was a threshing floor where a real, rooted yes could evolve into refined elements—materials with which we could design and express the best life art the two of us could manage for the sake of "God so loved the world that He gave His only begotten Son" (John 3:16 NKJV).

I'm using and choosing marriage as an illustration of one of the highest forms of art two people can cocreate, and this is about more than solid commitment and stellar communication. This is about the truth that marriage vows get torn a hundred ways to Sunday. Yet the work of art that is kingdom marriage doesn't go through the holy fire of crisis without being refined, restored, redeemed, and resurrected. That's because there lives a Marriage in this torn-asunder-love world worth reflecting, and our marriages can be mirrors held up in salute to it.

I see you sitting across from me, and I'm telling you straight and earnest now: the art of marriage is first about death and death and more death to self, about dying to viewpoints and ego and ideals we think are important so that our union can get born and born and reborn and resurrected from the cold ash of life's merciless fires. It's a fine art that micromodels art's very own Author so that which gets painted on the canvas of earth's landscape is something that's been brushed with strokes of cross and genius and our own squeezed-out heart's blood.

We, the artists of our own marriage, chose to put down our personal treasures and die by crucifixion so that the real work could be exalted; our uncommon, mutual, wedded cells were raised up to be a singularly crafted reflection of the Master Artist.

Taste and go deep now and gather all the morsels of your imagination. We're going to affirm the life that comes on the other side of death's door and the art that gets birthed when we choose to die while we're still alive.

Austin and I could rewrite the definition of *miracle* off the broken back of our story. Now here we are, fifteen years into our union, eight years since we began the uphill and arduous work of repairing and redeeming the art of ourselves. And the best part? The best part has been all the dates we made with death and how we dug our own graves to lie down in and how our individual and mutual dying became the fertile soil from which a small shoot of hope sprang forth to herald the resurrected work of pure, luminous art we were becoming.

The best part was learning from Jesus how to die on this side of the cemetery. We followed Jesus into the terrifying enterprise of allowing him to move us, change us, strip us down to the bare bones, and rebuild our bodies from the marrow out. It was (and is) a bloody business, to be sure, with the juice getting squeezed from our souls until there was nothing left except the waterless rind.

But resurrection was on the other side of suffering, or at least we hoped it was. We were prostrate and begging for the gospel truth to be true, the truth illustrated in the story of Jesus Christ that life was waiting on the other side of death, healing on the other side of scars and chaos, joy coming in the morning when the stones had been rolled away, true self birthed again and again while false self keeps dying.

It was a holy night when Austin and I celebrated our tenth wedding anniversary with a vow renewal ceremony—oh, holy ritual, with our holy heads bent in holy wonder. And even the streaming-free tears were salted with holy emotion that came in waves and weight because we had made it this far. And if ever a voice quiver can be holy, it was in this time and space when vow-words written in black, scrolled on white paper, were strongly and surely spoken into the grey shades of our reality. It was a reality that had known difficulty and decay and drama but had refused to let go of the wrestling until it was blessed with a new name and a long-lasting limp in the hip or shin or stomach. We could still feel its pain and remember.

That holy night we stood in the middle of an elbow-to-elbow circle of our twenty closest life companions and declared our repledges to each other. And wouldn't you know that heaven's holy hush drenched our air and drew out our senses to drag in the Spirit as she smoked the room with the floating whirl of her hovering presence. She glided and turned and dove and whooshed and arched and returned and thrummed around and between all our limbs and brushed over our skin in that sacred, hushed murmur of hers. And we felt transported to another galaxy altogether, a gentle place where a shielding barrier held us safe from the invasion of murk and dinge. Nothing nefarious was going to happen this holy night, not on her holy watch.

Our second vow ceremony was different than the rookie hooking of our youth because this time we knew. My precious Jesus, we knew what cards life could deal, and we knew that our own treacherous humanity could cheat with the hands we were dealt. We knew that vows designed to be kept get torn and busted a hundred contrary ways to Sunday. We knew all this—and more so beyond. And because of our knowing, our vow words that second time around meant shooting stars and whole high skies more and those redefined vow-words were ten years long and ten years deep and ten years burned through holy fire.

We knew, and we still stood on our holy legs of flesh with our hands clasped tight unto death and our eyes locked true for dear life. And we made our yes known down below to the core of the earth and up high to the throne room of heaven and to all living and deceased between.

We said yes again because we didn't go through holy fire without being scathed with refining burn marks—scars and char. We said yes again because restoration and redemption and resurrection became real and as necessary to us as the bread and breath that sustains our beings. We said yes because our belief in and intentions for marriage had evolved alongside our purification and came from a deeper place than the answers that come skimmed off the top: "I want to wake up every day with my best friend" or "two are better than one" or "he/she completes me."

After being affixed to someone for a decade, these reasons couldn't stand alone any longer. The crisis of our experience demanded that we have an exceptional reason for being joined and an exceptional reason for staying joined.

Why marriage? I had asked myself the evening before.

Because I would give my living and dying breath to reflect, in any way we artistically and possibly can, an image like the busted, bloody Christ. An image of a marriage that fairly screams out past the planets and moons and suns and stars and galaxies and down deep black holes and back to this blue and green sphere and right into the thickness of our human hearts, screams of a love so insurmountable, it's insurmountable. Here stands the deepest mystery of the universe that marriage contains and reflects.

When Austin and I refastened ourselves one to the other, it was with the intention that we, together, are a mirror of the risen Son on his wedding day. Our highest form of thanks for that gift is to return it with the soul of our marriage living outside our bodies in a well-thought-out and well-intentioned and beauty-driven artistic expression of incarnation and image. And we, the marriage artists, will continue to die so that our work can serve that Work.

Have you ever thought of your marriage (or future marriage) as art, a canvas you can stretch and restretch and paint over and scrape off layers from and do those colors again?

What are the elements—the media—that you have at your disposal to do this work?

What does it look like to create a work of marriage art that reflects the combined souls of you and your partner and the work of the great Artist?

Being bound together in marriage means taking part in the most vulnerable and fragile sacrament under the sun, and you and yours and me and mine must aim to be extra tender with our eggshell status. We must drop and drop before Christ and supplicate for guidance and protection and more love than either of us can muster. We must practice every method we can think of to help cover and care for our crackability.

But what about all the cracks you and I already have? Well the light just beams through and through them and really brightly, too, with blinding rays and iridescent prisms of color. So let's just keep those fractures and let our married love shine.

19

PARENTING AS ART

If an artist is a servant to the work, then by and for all that's holy I want to be lifted up by my armpits and gotten out of the way. I want to bend at nothing less than my waistline and my lower appendages, too, and with all my ethos and animalism go low, totally bowed over in surrender to what needs to get made. Because, as I've already said, our collected and combined and intertwined art is how God is enfleshed and becomes visible on our sphere. This is how the Baby gets pushed out over and over into the shadowy nights, our painful acts of surrender producing living masterpieces. (Do you believe it?)

For what it's worth, this principle applies to our babies too.

Have you ever thought of parenting as a work of art?

This chapter is for all you parents and soon-to-be parents and parent figures—anyone who goes to the depths and heights and back again and again while nurturing and raising children. You have my heart especially because I am one of you. A prodigious portion of my personal work at this juncture of my life involves bringing up our three kids alongside my husband (and our community). And my commitment to them is not just as a mother, but as an artist too.

Did you catch that? I'm committed to being both a parent and an artist when it comes to the shaping and shifting and building and developing of our young ones. The three of them are my most challenging and costly (and interactive) canvas.

The strokes and textures and mixing of media that go into this work must be done with my face against the cellar floor— the lowest point in our house that I can go before summoning the humility and the courage to go back up and brush another singular streak across the unique spread of the child's life.

In other words, I don't just want to parent for parenting's sake; I want to bend before the task with an avant-garde spirit, grasp the tools of alchemy and anthropology between my trembling fists, and originate something totally unique to who I am and who we are and what we're sanctioned for as a family.

Parenting is drudgery sometimes and downright gear-grinding half the days of every week, but most of all parenting is art—praise the Powers. And how do you and I kneel and become obedient before the art of rearing our sons and daughters, cultivating flesh for the express purpose of watching original masterpieces come forth and shine like stars in the universe, each holding out his or her only, only, only—one and only—rare light?

We need to remember what we have to work with, remember that within the nonframework of avant-garde any kind of creation is possible, that the artistic components you have at your fingertips are nothing less than the plasma and cartilage and sinew and skin and soul, and that alchemy, too, rests in the Spirit's featherless wings and waits for you. Mix your "anything can happen" attitude with all your very own elements, and see what results.

It was a Wednesday, and I stopped and dropped in the middle of putting clean sheets on the master bed because the weight of my world had crashed in a heap upon my shoulders. I remember pressing my palms open against the mattress, my back arched like a crescent moon, my heavy head hanging listless between my shoulder blades.

In no uncertain terms I told the Great Ones that they'd made a mistake. That surely having three boys within three years of one another and then homeschooling them—plus this, plus that and the other thing—was too much weight for any one person to stand up under. More specifically, I was living on the north side of way too much noise and activity for a certified introvert who craves solitude and stillness and quiet more than all the known things on the whole globe.

Then I remembered that God only gives us what we could never handle on our own. And with that recollection of truth, the brine-like water broke free from my eyelids and spilled onto the bedsheets I was hunched over. I spoke aloud to the Wind in the room, weeping something along the lines of "I don't have what it takes to be a mom, and my back feels all busted-up here, and while we're on the subject, I need a wee bit more wisdom than just the size of Tinkerbell's left arse cheek."

To be more specific with you, we had been desperate to comprehend how to navigate and nurture our oldest son, who was transitioning from boyhood into young manhood with the sudden show of adolescent hormones rushing mighty river-style through his unsuspecting body. From the lips of a grandma, who years earlier, had sidled up to my grocery cart full of small kids and consumables, I'd heard the admonition that the hormones and whatnot would appear some day. But I'd been really dumb enough to think it would never happen to us, that we would somehow be exempt from teenage tensions if we tended and trained the boys just right.

I've been wrong more times than New York City has yellow taxis, but I've almost never been more wrong than I was with that silly and stupidly naive assumption. Nature is a strong and equal contender to nurture.

Our boy, Gabe, can put a finger on the day when he started feeling different. And by "different" I mean someone replaced the insides of our child with an alien snorting haywire.

Before I go any further with this story, I want to disclose that Gabriel has given me full permission to call him an alien, haywire, and otherwise. He knows he's an alien as often as I'm an idiot and everyone else is also a butthead (his words—glad we cleared that up). Plus he said, "If telling my story will help someone, then I don't care." We've all decided to own our junk in this house.

For whatever reason, Gabe's poor body had been besieged with a bigger-than-average battalion of tormenting stimulants that triggered repeated and disproportionate displays of anger. This anger could get ignited from just one tiny little sniffle coming from the unsuspecting nostril of a brother sitting next to him on the couch. And no amount of reasoning or deep breathing or threatened consequences was enough sometimes to pull Gabe out of his sudden hysteric reaction.

Later, when the cooldown finally came and he stepped into the eye of his own hurricane, with tears and sorrow and confusion and all the rest, he always, always, always made the most meek and riven apology to each family member he'd violated. He had also started praying every day of his own volition that God would help him not react so aggressively to his frequently pesky little brothers or to any other person or thing that might get an immediate rise out of him—like me or Austin or the frozen computer.

Gabriel and I were having a post-fraternal-war conversation one day, and with cry-streaks all over his cheeks and emotion throttling his throat, he said to me, "Mama, I'd rather be able to change than have a million dollars. I don't understand why God isn't helping me."

I'll go ahead and confess to you that my heart ached so far it split to slivers while witnessing my son plead for a transformation that felt so far-reaching for him, especially since he'd been praying for what feels to him like a very long time. Gabe wanted change more than anything, but he couldn't seem to stop the blowing up and blowing apart and making storms inside himself and our home. We all ached together.

That's the gist of our repetitive struggles. And by "repetitive" I mean more than once every day. And just one of these situations (read: volcano eruptions) would leave me entirely wrung dry and all used up, like I needed to take a nap into next week. Not to mention how tired I was of hearing myself talk in all the "teachable moments" that didn't seem to teach anything.

I was tired. Gabe was tired. We all were tired. And that's the situation that brought me to my moment on the mattress. The bedroom became my confessional that day as I cried out to heaven, worn down into the most stretched-out shred of myself. I prayed about things mentioned and things unmentioned. But what brought me the most despair was not knowing how to help my son through his tumultuous transitions.

Faithful like the sunrise, Gabriel's anger came back the very next day, and with wild eyes and clenched fists he tornadoed around his brother for barely any reason at all. I was in the kitchen, elbow deep in sugar-cookie dough, when the tyrant tune reached my ears. And the first thing I did this time was breathe. I sucked down all the deep breaths I possibly could and whispered half-a-dozen "Oh God, help me" prayers before calling my angry son to "come here please."

Quietly I asked him to go somewhere alone just until I could wash my hands and come talk to him. The good Lord knows I didn't need time to wash my hands. I needed time to wash my heart so I could enter into a space with my son where I could see beyond the regularly expressed surface issue. And I consciously wondered if now was a time and space to get out my tools and start a new art piece for our family parenting gallery.

I don't remember how long I stood at the kitchen sink, beseeching the great Artist and waiting motionless and silent for an extra scrap of inspiration to fall from the sky. And inspiration did finally fall. My mind was filled with the light of an entirely new nurturing technique to try with our son, a technique I'd never read about or heard of.

It was worth a try.

I grabbed this idea and rushed headlong and excited to meet Gabe in his bedroom, where he was already quieted down. Clutching his hand tightly in mine, I looked into his teary, tender eyes and asked if we could experiment together. He let me guide his body gently to lie down on the rug, where I positioned his arms and legs and head in the most relaxed pose, placed one of my palms on his forehead and one on his stomach, and felt the Wind literally whoosh in on the wings of my urgent pleas.

Because I didn't want to forget a single atom of that experience, what follows is the record I scribed in my journal the moment I finished ministering to my boy:

Me: Okay, bub. Close your eyes and take five deep breaths all the way down to your belly. Breathe slow and long. Relax your face. Loosen your limbs.

(One-minute pause while Gabe stills down.)

Me: While you continue to breathe and keep your eyes closed, I want you to tell me where your anger is located in your body. Is it in your mind? Or your heart? Or your stomach? Is it in your left thigh? (Seriously, you never know.)

Without hesitation, Gabe says: "The anger is in my stomach." At this point my hands feel like they're lit with fire, and I move both heated palms to rest softly on his bare belly.

> **Me:** Okay, the anger is in your stomach. What does it feel like?
> **Gabe:** My stomach feels tight and really tense. It hurts all over.
> **Me:** Okay, we know the anger is in your stomach and is making your stomach tense and painful. Now I want you to imagine the anger in your stomach and tell me what it looks like.
> **Gabe:** It looks like a dark, red cloud.
> **Me:** Imagine for me this dark, red cloud sitting in your belly and occupying all this space where it doesn't belong. (Pause) Do you see it?
> **Gabe:** Yes.
> **Me:** Now picture this dark, red cloud being sucked out of your belly until it's all the way gone.

Immediately following this instruction, Gabriel's eyes pop open in surprise, and he exclaims: "How did you do that? I can't believe it! My stomach hurt so bad, and now it's all gone. It's a miracle!"

I'm totally astonished and not astonished at all and smiling to split my face at his gushed-forth wonder and joy.

I tell him, "Hang on a second; we're not done yet. Close your eyes and imagine the space in your stomach where all that anger was. Now that it's gone, you have all this emptiness inside you, and I want you to envision it. Do you see it?"

Gabe: Yes.
Me: All right, now that you have this empty space, you need to fill it back up with something. What do you want to fill it back up with?
Gabe: God's love. I want to fill it with God's love.
Me: Oh, good. That's beautiful, Gabe. What does God's love look like to you?
Gabe: God's love looks like Jesus' face.
Me: Okay. Imagine Jesus' face coming to you and filling all the empty places inside your stomach.

And that's what Gabriel does. He gathers the floating molecules of Jesus' face and pulls them together and tucks them right inside himself, filling the chasm the anger once occupied. And with so much gladness and gratitude sweeping in soft ripples off his skin and out his soul-windows, my boy throws his adolescent arms around my neck and fervently whispers against my face, "Thank you so much, Mama. I feel free!" And this newly renewed mama murmurs back, "Oh, honey, Jesus set you free. I just made my hands and my heart available to him."

As I walked away from that experience on the rug in Gabe's room, my whole cellular body was buzzing from tip to top. I had let myself be used in every nth way, wrung out for the sake of my son and the Spirit, and the result had been something profound and eternal—a jointly created masterpiece. Something beautiful had been created because I took a meditative, listening stand at my kitchen sink. I'd listened long enough to hear the Alchemist guide me toward something new, an unorthodox method of parenting that had left Gabe and me both healed of the fractures we'd been carting around for weeks. The game had changed, and the elements turned into art because the I in me had managed to get out of the way.

I'm still a little in awe of what was created that day.

I learned there are times when what an acting-out child needs most isn't time-outs or privileges revoked or firm words or extra chores. Sometimes the transgressor needs to be touched where he or she is hurting most. And maybe at times being a parent is less about correction and more about offering ourselves as clay vessels of healing for our children and for ourselves too.

Gabe didn't receive a magic, once-and-for-all cure that day. But for the twenty minutes we spent on the floor that night, all was well. It was like we were removed to an alternate universe, one without a clock ticking down time or that list of things to be done. Instead, there was only closeness, my boy, and communion with the healing power of love.

As I said, a masterpiece.

Gabe and I and the Spirit made something together that day we'll never forget, something that got written into the threads of eternity.

✳

What became most apparent to me after that experience was that the opportunities for artistic endeavor in parenting are endless.

Not every method and technique has been discovered. Not every possible approach has been passed on or written down. There are still a million nuanced ways to nurture our children that have never been explored before—a million different ways to recombine the basic materials of bone and flesh and experience and love into living masterpieces.

Parenting as an art form is not only a value that transforms our own family relationships. Continually and beautifully expressed, it can be an attractive and compelling invitation for the outside world to view the parent-kid connections in a new light. Other families will be drawn to the ways in which you manifest your canvas.

Most important, because children learn by watching and imitating, every beautiful intention and devotion to our young ones teaches them to become artists themselves. Maternal or paternal love can be their aviary until the doors are swung wide and they go aerial—up, up, and away. And with the Spirit unfurling our thought and creativity, we can make priceless, timeless art together.

20

SPIRITUALITY AS ART

What does it mean to have an abounding and beautiful and bright spiritual life? How do we connect and commune with They who are greater and higher and other and all around so much more than us?

As evidenced by all the spiritual practices we've seen people exercise throughout history in their devoted attempts to get themselves closer to the divine, men and women around the globe have been asking and answering these questions since the beginning of time.

For some people spiritual engagement involves a church service inside a sanctuary. For others it's a hike up a mountain or a prayer walk by the river. Some find spiritual connection in an hour of chanting and meditation after work or a weekly sharing of communion around the kitchen table with friends or daily yoga next to the rising dawn or a week of fasting food or a lifestyle of celibacy.

My mom regularly makes a banquet for homeless people as a way of exercising her connection with the divine. Farmers have been known to employ their tractors and cornfields as part of their highest spiritual routines. And Native Americans say that there is no temple better than creation in which to commune with the "One who may be met face to face in the mysterious, shadowy aisles of the primeval forest, or on the sunlit bosom of virgin prairies."[1]

Sometimes it's a million different practices from one day to the next that contribute to make a whole spiritual experience.

When I was growing up, a large part of my spirituality was defined by going to church on Sunday mornings and Wednesday evenings and meeting in small groups and having quiet times and going to Bible studies and potlucks. I also read Christian books and listened to Christian music and used Christian lingo and made sure my skirt fell nearly to my kneecaps.

None of these customs were (or are) inherently bad or incorrect. But my church experience was based on conformity, on following the rules, on duplicating in myself the brand of Christianity that surrounded me. If you were a Christian, I assumed, then this was what your spiritual life looked like and this was how you acted and these were the exact letters to quantify your speech pattern.

Personalized spirituality wasn't talked about or celebrated in my corporate Christian context. (Actually, as a young woman, I never would've even used the word *spirituality* because to my mind it was somehow associated with Eastern religious practice.) I never heard a preacher in a pulpit sermonize on the merits and wisdom of designing a completely rare and artistic spiritual expression using the ingredients of my relationship with Jesus and the wild anthem of my own soul.

However, my perspective has changed over the years, and

what I understand spirituality to be now is a little different, a little simpler, and swings the door wide open for endless manifestations of artistic spiritual rhythms.

Christian spirituality as I understand it aims to reconcile our bodies with the image of God as personified by Jesus. Spirituality is being animated, being lit up from within by Christ and his upside-down kingdom. Jesus showed us through the incarnation that the physical world is an ideal place for us to encounter the divine. And because we claim that Jesus lives within us and that we are now his real hands and feet and heart living on the earth today, it's safe to conclude that aspect of our lives is, in a very real sense, filled with spiritual significance. In short: spirituality is what I would call practicing heaven right now. To quote Catherine of Siena again, "All the way to heaven is heaven because [Jesus] said 'I am the way.'"

Similarly, Jesuit leader Pedro Arrupe relates spirituality to the experience of falling in love:

> Nothing is more practical than finding God, than falling in love in a quite absolute way, final way. What you are in love with, what seizes your imagination, will affect everything. It will decide what will get you out of bed in the morning, what you do with your evenings, how you will spend your weekends, what you read, who you know, what breaks your heart, and what amazes you with joy and gratitude. Fall in love, stay in love, and it will decide everything.[2]

Living and loving and waking and walking and every piece and particle of existence in between are ideally designed to be spiritual acts. Nothing is separate. All life is a sacred act of worship—or it can be.

Going to Goodwill before Halloween to buy costumes for the kids can be a sacred act.

So can picking out fruit and eggs at the farmer's market on Saturday mornings, serving scoops of food at the soup kitchen on Tuesday nights, or going to the movies on Friday with a group or friends or all alone.

Taking a shower can be a spiritual act of cleansing.

Hand-washing the dishes can remind us of baptism and resurrection.

Every single moment of our lives holds the potential for a spiritual connection, but we must decide to open ourselves to that potential—open our eyes, listen for the Wind, bring Jesus into any given moment. We have the freedom to choose how our acts of worship play out before God and before others. How we do that is what makes our individual, unique spirituality a form of art. It is our greatest work, the river that flows into and supplies everything.

It takes intention and discipline on our part to be awake and avant-garde enough to welcome alchemy and the elements of anthropology and create something spiritually artful with them. But the intention and discipline needed to stay awake and active in hallowed communion with God are worth the effort because such communion harbors our souls and develops healthy, true selves. Without close union we quickly succumb to staleness and fear and are easily seduced by lies and systems and whatever else isn't real.

Being spiritually awake is our birthright, an antidote to untruth and the hope of heaven for us while we're in exile.

Each of us is connected to the Source uniquely. The intersection of our very own innate elements and the pure, limitless synergy of the Spirit creates an exclusive spiritual bond unlike anyone else's. Do you believe it?

The Father and I move to music in a mode that nobody else in the world ever will because my DNA is absolutely different—the Source honors the specific, intricate knit of my body, mind, and soul. He knows I'm unique, and he would never dishonor my thisness by making me conform to the prescribed pattern of someone else.

The specific way we sway and spin and light on fire and make love is a kind of spiritual art that no one else has or does. And I will use every trick and tool I've got to allow myself to go quieter and sink into us deeper than I think possible, because this relationship is the apex of my presented art and the roots by which all my fruits are fed.

Being with God, I've found, is very much like practicing heaven right now.

So I pour myself over and over and over an ancient manger in every radical way I can imagine, and I am a midwife that ushers forth incarnation. I pour myself out even though the thought of showing the world my love for him feels at least vastly vulnerable, as if I were the one spreading my legs for all the world to see while contracting the crown of God's head into the hay.

But if ever there is time and space for vulnerability, it's alongside the memory and truth of Christ coming to us amniotic and squalling and bald. To me, this invokes all the base and crooked worshipers to come as defenseless and displayed as possible before the flesh-born King.

Do you have perceptions of God that actually block your ability to create an artistic spiritual rhythm with him (or her)?

Brennan Manning is known for saying, "You're only going to be as big as your own concept of God."[3] For example, if you believe that God is fundamentally petty or punitive or distant or narrow-minded, this view will greatly affect the creative spiritual work you put out into the universe. Your work will be petty, narrow-minded, punitive, and unfriendly.

But if your view of God is defined by the kind of immeasurable love exhibited between the stable and Calvary, then there is no end to what you can artistically do because immeasurable love is a well that won't run dry.

Your spiritual life and the artistic expression of it are determined by your view of the divine. So who do you believe God to be? What do you see in your mind's eye when you contemplate him? It matters, because who the Great Mystery is to you determines and informs everything else.

When you look at the stable, do you see the Baby?

The weary world waits and anticipates, but mostly it simply suffocates, drowning from life lived in bloodshot centuries of drunken contortion, demonized distortion, debauchery of global proportion. We've had pain in our bellies and a propensity for doom and despair, and finally, from the darkness of a virgin's birth canal, there came a big and bursting light.

An infant is born in stable shadows with floating dust-dots and the large, moist eyes of cattle looking on with a confession of beastly affection. There is the odor alongside, and maybe you can smell it? The metallic tang of vital fluids meets the funk of body sweat to mingle down next to the dung heaps, and the starstruck shepherds and strange sorcerers crest the easterly hill, and nothing is ever the same again. And I must go there, too, on this regular pilgrimage of the soul, this pilgrimage across the desert of my Gentile heart to meet with my diapered King. Because it only took infinity poured into infancy to take away my iniquity.

And while you're away in a manger, can I lie down next to you? Flesh-to-flesh in a peasant's feed trough with your heaven-sent, celestial-scented baby breath bathing my earthen pores. I would curl myself next to your lowly born story and hold you against my cheek-grazing lips, hold the Baby that bound me together in my own mother's womb. I would hold you in the skin-itching straw under the looking stars in the night sky, and I would smell you—just there, in the crease of your cosmic neck. We're so tight together, tears aren't temptation; they're a torrent. My lashes drip, and I can feel the tiny tick of your heart flutter.

Am I near enough here to know you better?

And would you know that this is my spiritual art? My way of transporting my spirit to be with my Lover in all the shapes and arrangements and designs I see him in—Baby first, then . . .

When you look at the cross, do you see the Man?

I've had thirty-four revolutions around this one cross, and for at least a lot of them I've beseeched the grown man strung up against the splinters and wood—with his Humpty Dumpty body all cracked to pieces and damaged badly and held together by rail nails—to let me come nearer and touch and taste and trace the tissue and textiles of myself along the ripped and warm and wet, red scars.

Maybe my cheek just reaches the end of his stem, and I fit his slippery foot in the hollow between my cheekbone and chin, and my face is suddenly streaked and scarlet. And there I stay to worship and give thanks with all the sincerity my fickle heart can manage on a dark and alluring day—dark because we have walked in a land so black we couldn't see our arms outstretched, and alluring because he broke through with the light of a million suns and suddenly shined upon us. And who would wonder why I want to aim my lips to kiss his bloody feet?

I will forever follow Jesus even if I end up cast up next to him on some kind of my own cross, because beyond my own cross I believe my heart's desire awaits. So I am foolish enough to come near.

When you feel your own breath coming up your lungs, or when you go outside and touch the air, do you see the Wind?

I know the way the Spirit inhabits my soul and breathes on me with the merciful breeze of a lovestruck swain, how she draws my specific tendrils out of the confines of my walls and blows strands of my soul into places that matter, then brings me home and wraps me in velvet blankets of herself. How she holds me tight for dear life and bottles my tears and triumphs and turns everything to everlasting gold.

She is my nearest friend, and I would throw the whole of all my parts at her just to see how wild and wonderful and free we can be together, making heaven explode to earth like dandelion fireworks or snowdrops erupting from the hard winter ground.

When you're sitting in silence with your eyes closed, contemplating on the Father, do you see the way he holds you?

Abba Father is the One who pulls my weight up and curves

me to fit in the furrow of his crisscrossed legs. I am on his lap sometimes and all my intestines soften like wax, go smooth and soft and warm with his exhaling next to my ear and his big palm pressing my child-sized head against the swelling and compressing of his immense chest.

I hear him whisper how he loves me first and finest and whispers in shades of holy and hidden mysteries, and I steep in the shelter that's under the cover of his broad and strong wings. This is where begins my true north and the direction I set my sails in, and together is when we coast our voyages into uncharted seas and settings and suns.

This imaginative "teleporting" is something I do to be closer to the One my soul longs for, and you can go to the Source in your own way too. You can make your spiritual life into the best and greatest work of art you will ever create. I wish upon a beaming and glittery Bethlehem star that you could make love with God—the Baby, the Man, the Spirit, the Father—in your own singular and not-supposed-to-be-the-same-as-anyone-else's way.

Meet the Great Silence alone and listen for the spiritual rhythms that are only yours. Make spiritual art; display it outside your body for the purpose of being an offering that interlocks with the great circle of contribution. All held up together, our created works reflect the glorious face of the divine. This is the greatest art and has the potential to magnetize all humankind unto the Maker, to sweep them off their feet and capture their souls.

Are we going to be obedient to the artwork of our lives for beautiful and beloved Christ's sake and the sake of kingdom come on earth as in heaven? Are we going to be careful with the artwork of our lives because it appears we only get a single shot on the whole precious and puzzling and perilous planet?

Side by side we can rock and croon over the Baby or kneel and feel the Man or ebb and flow with the Wind or curl up on the Father's lap in the ways that each of us only can, with the uniquely expressed spiritual art of our singular hearts.

21

DO YOU BELIEVE IT?

I hope these pages have been a place for your soul to breathe, expand like pregnancy, and rethink the shape and size and singularity of what you've been made of. We've all got the same stuff swirling around inside us, and we are also all vastly different, with our weird shadings of that same stuff.

Have you begun to identify and separate yourself from the things that aren't you? One or two systems or shoulds, formulas, demands, rackets, or how-tos that were never meant to be a part of your special, sacred blend? Or maybe you've been mimicking someone at the expense of your own sparkle. These parasites are cheap substitutes; leeches that suck the truth from your inherent parts.

It's okay to get free. You will find what you seek if you seek for it with all your heart.

You are embroidered from the sparkling stars in his irises and the holy zephyr pushing forth from its lungs—star flecks and Spirit-breath. Multiply that by billions and we are a glittering galaxy that looks like one beautiful and broken body, for better or for worse. Christ who puts us each together in one piece, whose very breath and blood flow through us, has destined it so.

Our favorite kingdom is not of this conformist world. This is good news because in this kingdom we are encouraged to come as we've been uniquely gifted to come, not just with all the humors and holes of our humanity, but with the exclusive DNA of our divinity too.

I hope your true self ignites and burns hot with the axiom of your own avant-garde heritage. You weren't made for conformity. You weren't made with some cosmic cookie cutter. You were made precious and rare and only.

You were made to bandersnatch.

A bandersnatch, remember, is someone who has decided to jump into the belief that his or her skin is singular, that his or her soul has a distinct and thoughtfully designed truth to it. In order to remain authentic to that conviction, bandersnatches must approach life with their very own unconventional habits and attitudes.

So walk into the next room or into a single moment tomorrow or no later than next Tuesday and inhale the air of the great Nonconformist. Look for opportunities to intend and make with the epidermis of your unorthodox fingers.

Be you. Be you. Be you. Be you.

It is so important just to be the avant-garde you. Blaze an original thought or a new rhythm or a trail through an unmarked forest—leave us a sign for the way you didn't go. It is your birthright to experiment and dare and pioneer as if the sole boundary holding you is the love you are guided by.

The hypnosis and immaturity of mainstream culture can't hold a candle to your particular path. Arch your neck, set your face to the promised land, shout your purposes to the atmosphere.

Or sit quietly in the corner and create a quilt like there's no pattern . . . or whose colors speak your unprecedented name.

I hope your receptors are on high alert, positioned for currents, stretched to sense more alchemy than before your other days. The Holy Specter literally pushes over you and in on you, and your corners and crevices and creases don't have to stand a chance against this waterfall of Spirit matter—say yes.

Alchemy is seriously, fiercely attempting not to be missed by you. Bend before nothing and give thanks. You've been gifted with the eyes to see that Something is actually there. Kiss the ground for the love of all things holy as you gaze up into air; the great Mystery is thrumming on the surface and in the depths, on your lips and in your lungs too, propelling anointed oxygen in and out. Alchemy is sitting between every solid, created thing, available and waiting to transmute every situation and story. *Lead us to what we should see.*

I hope you supplicate the "Teach me how to love" prayers and that you're growing the comet-sized heart of an anthropologist. May your eyes be so spacious, so tender, so full of love that you see every grain of sand, every newborn babe, every wildflower and wacko as worthy of all the honor and dignity and kindness you can muster up from the bottom of your being.

The stuff of earth is handmade by the One who blew it into existence with the bang of his breath. Hold it soft and tender between your hands and unwrap each piece and person like it's Christmas morning.

The expressed combination of your communion with the divine plus your DNA plus your own avant-garde approach to life plus the infinite elements of air and earth combine to create your art, your soul outside your body. Your art expresses you and offers back to the world a gift that makes known the kingdom that is "not of this world" (John 18:36 NKJV). Incarnate the supernatural kingdom by any and all loving and creative means available to you. Let's paint seeds to plant and grow change, stripes across the sky for everyone to see and be inspired by.

Do you know why I aimed to press every theme, every idea, every letter through the filter of what I understand this other-worldly kingdom to be saying? The earth is only on its way to being set right. *We* are only on our way to being set right, and Jesus is the Way for us to learn alignment. Kingdom come means that our bodies and the dust we stand on are in the process of being saved, being reconciled to who Jesus is and the kind of domain he demonstrated. This is participating in heaven like we don't even have to wait. Bring it now. Make art that looks like a lodestar for the kingdom. Incarnate an entirely new way of doing life.

I'm inviting you to what you were made for.

Again and again I say this because this otherworldly king-dom that we entreat to come is the same kingdom that will break the people free from the systems of a dying world, the systems that suffocate and squeeze the life air and lifeblood from the gasping bodies we inhabit. Our poor, gasping bodies know what they were made for, and it's not the rules and rot and lies that we've been listening to—do this and do that, stand up and sit down and walk in a straight line, for Pete's sake, and buy me and you'll be happy, and you should have so much variety in your closet, and keep up with the Joneses, and watch the tabloids for what's important.

We've paid for so many systems with our own life-dripping blood. It isn't funny at all, and we wonder why we have zero energy left with which to make life-giving art. I'll tell you again why: we've contracted too much of it away for the abso-lutes of nothing.

Check through everything you hold true and ask if it's

actually real. Hold it up against this gospel truth: our bodies were made for—and only for—two words in all the known galaxies, and—I'm saying this again too—those two words are simply, profoundly, hauntingly, "Follow me."

"Follow me."

Follow him in the opposite direction and away from the human-made systems and shoulds and supposed-tos and successes that abuse and murder your inborn art, that kill your precious, organic soul. And if what you hold dear doesn't align with the "Follow me" of a reverse kingdom, it might be contributing to your own slow death.

Kingdom come, I say. because when Jesus walked this old firmament, this world full of heartbreak and injustice and violence and buffoons and bafflement, everything he did and said, every way he acted and every word he spoke scribed a universal code into the web of the cosmos as if to say:

This is the way life is. And please, for the love of all important and beautiful things, watch my feet and watch my hands and watch my eyes. Because this, this, this is really the way life is. Follow me into the mud and spit of the world and do something magical with it. Follow me into the mustard seed and mountain-moving moments. Follow me as I chase after the idiots and misfits and mongrels (the last shall be first). Stand on your head, and you will begin to see. Follow me into the sharing of what you have and watch the miracle of multiplication happen, the masses getting fed with endless baskets of bread and fish. Follow me into the art of dying on your own cross so your true self can be resurrected alongside my busted body. Follow me.

Only a fool would heed his voice.

As in: a fool for Christ's sake is the wisest course you could plot and plow.

As in: a fool for Christ's sake is the new wise man who still adores the One born in Bethlehem.

Jesus came to give us the gift of learning how to live, learning who we are and what we were made for. And the most artful thing we could ever do is actually just follow him in our own diverse and peculiar ways. Herein lies the way in which your character and art acquires terrain—hills and valleys, depths and heights.

I know I asked you in the beginning, and I'm asking you again at the end:

Within the framework of being a child of God, do you know what part of God you represent?

Do you know where you begin and where you end or the here-to-here of your uniqueness?

Life is not about shaping an alternate identity for ourselves or borrowing pieces of other people's individuality in substitute for what we don't understand about ourselves. It's about discovering the identity we already have. It's about connecting the dots and following the threads that move us inch by inch closer to the blinding reality of our true selves.

Do you hear the silent, holy voice of heaven ringing with urgency and a need for your identity to be visible on the earth?

Remember that your constitutional design is the most natural part of you, but it's also the part of you that literally can't breathe or bloom under all the layers of cultural conformity. Don't let the great blaring voices of conventional culture own you with their oppressive systems anymore. If a system is just, it will still have room for the surprise of the Holy Spirit. It will be rooted in the natural law of an eternal Being and will uplift and support your true self—make you extraordinarily soar. If a system is unjust, it will depress and degrade your divine personality. (In many situations, *system* is another word for lie.)

Self-discovery will not rotate on the wheels of inevitability; it will come from your resolute efforts to be cosearchers, co-laborers, and cocreators with the Spirit. There is treasure in the field still, and we can find it, especially if we push past the tangle of fear, pull on our muck boots, and go out together, getting lower and lower and lower than our knees, stuffing both fists in the dirt and digging down deep to the roots of things, where mysteries of selfhood reside and practically cry forth to be found.

Are you ready and willing to do the good and hard work of stripping and extracting the vacuous systems and labels that humanity has thrust upon you and watch the language for your uncommon inner workings bloom like magic?

You are desired, so let down your hair or pull it back—whatever you need to do to get the kingdom in your two clumsy mitts and make something of it. Bring it, transmute it, reveal it through your creative work. Step back from the canvas of your life every now and again and say to the Great Ones, *Here's my priceless gift to you and to your kingdom and to the world, as silly and aching and profound as it may be. I've been told the contributions of my identity fill a hole in the universe.*

I want you to believe it because, though you be faceless to me, I can imagine you still, and you are my family. In some how and in some way your joy and wholeness are linked to mine. We are bound together, tied to one another's ribs and pits and cartilage and craniums for better or for worse.

I believe it. Now, let's pull off the boots we've been trekking in, enjoy a cup of something, and have this conversation: It might be nearly impossible to fully remove yourself from the oppressive systems and chronic cultural customs that are in the mix of you and that you are in the mix of too. But I do believe it's important work to begin investing in the practice of identifying and extracting the ones that lord over and squash your specific animation and contribution. Remove the nonsupportive systems so you can reenter the institutionalized landscape and redefine the terms from a renewed point of view. (This is kingdom come.)

Ask yourself these questions to get you started:

How do you create in such a way that engages with the traditions, while remaining true to the uniqueness of your creative work?

Who would you be and what would you create if you weren't afraid?

What would you say?

How would you live?

What are some things you would do differently if you didn't feel the pressure to conform to traditions or systems?

What bits of heaven and the bits of earth would you combine right now to make kingdom-advancing life art?

Watch your life for the answers to your own questions. And if you don't like the answers, if you find that you don't like the direction your feet take you or the things you put your hands to, then commit to changing the game or changing the channel or changing the music or turning the blasted, befuddled tables. Lay down on your own flat back in a space made for questions and beseech the Almighty like your whole self is burning from that one word and punctuation: *How?*

How do I change anything, let alone myself?

How do I dismantle and bump and knock things around enough inside me that pieces begin to break loose and I get free?

Alchemy is there—peel back your distractions and consumptions, your mind wars and whatnots and listen for as long as it takes to hear one thing, one response to one question at a time. It's all our bodies can handle anyway.

It might be tempting to take the content and stories of

Bandersnatch and fully adopt the patterns I've outlined. But I would encourage you to take the principles alone into the creating room of your own soul, have a meeting with the Spirit there, and cut yourself loose—you wild and mythical, uncommon and unconventional creature, you. Have fun and be free and throw off any norms or earth-made systems or status quos that you've exchanged emotional real estate for. Take it back like it's yours.

Start over from the bottom up if need be or from the top down, unless sideways is better for you. Release yourself to recover your natural-made instincts, to find who it is you truly are underneath all the layers of illusion the world has heaped on you.

Be you be you be you—part myth, all truth, wholly adored.

Come closer to me, brother, sister. It's nearly our last page together, and I have a capacity for intimacy and an impulse to be near you. My spirit addresses your spirit; I don't know how to be far away. Let's say something important, as if time is relentlessly clicking, draining grain by grain from an hourglass and we haven't laughed enough, cried enough, raced spread-wide through open spaces enough, lived enough. "One wild and precious life"[1] is hardly enough, and dare I say it's still precious and wild and exceptional even when it's numbing, breaking, monotonous, and fundamentally mundane.

Nothing within these pages is meant to be a formula to drink or a blueprint to pursue because I don't believe that your inherent design wants—or functions best with—rigid umbrella answers or neat equations that take the place of your own belly-born originality. I hope you'll be enriched and inspired, but your birthright is to engage with the mess of it, to make a dozen million mistakes and trip over more edges than you have days in your life. No matter how seemingly small and insignificant you might think it is, what you have to offer is acutely essential. Please put forth your trembling, sanctified work and fill the body.

Go before the vastness with your approaches and elements, knowing that more than half the battle is believing the truth of what you were born for. You are a creator; do you believe it? And if you believe it, where will your unfettered feet go? What will your unclenched fists do? How will your heart and soul and whole body transform your daily life making? Because it's your feet and your hands and the direction you take your body that will tell the story of what you believe and value.

Present yourself before the Living One in all your knit-together uniqueness, in all your strangeness, your peculiarity, your one and only youness. Go into the wilderness, go into the feckless and ferocious and fascinating throes of the globe and make something, anything for Christ's sake. Even on those days when you can't perceive him (we all have those), do your gosh-darn best to take the flesh and foliage and all the stuff of earth within the reach of your fingertips and believe that he is with you, that he desires you to cocreate, and that the stuff of heaven only waits for your yes.

At the end of this day and tomorrow, too, and forever as well, your art is less for other people and more for the love of God. (That's not to say we don't hope our souls touch one another in some penetrating and precious way.) If you hold tight to that axiom, then you are free from the need to be esteemed, extolled, honored, or praised for the work that you make. You'll be free from the fears of humiliation, vulnerability, ridicule, and rejection. It's for the love of God that you create, for the love of the interlocking circle of contribution that reveals the whole of Christ's body.

Do you believe it?

ACKNOWLEDGMENTS

I've heard it said that it takes a village to raise a child. Well, it also takes a village to make a book and without the support of my people, this work would not have been born.

Every iota of my "thanks" goes first to you, my Muse, the holy one born in Israel. I am breath of your breath, blood of your blood, body of your body.

Austin, you are the uncontended love of my earthly life, and it is not lip service to say that I wouldn't be who I am today without all the yesterdays spent with you. And I'm so grateful that all your tomorrows are mine.

Gabe, Seth, and Jude—my favorite, always bubs—I'm so proud to be your mama. Thank you for having the patience and fortitude to allow me to grow up on you.

Mama and Papa, I wouldn't trade a single part of either of you or our story for anything ever, period.

My siblings and their spouses, I'm counting on many more mountaintop adventures and late-night laughter. We're the best together and I am most myself in your company. Glory.

My dear New Haven people, what can I honestly say? You are my tribe. A place I call home, like warm fires and Christmas morning. You've been with me through the best of times and the worst of times; you have seen my crazy and my amazing, and you have never stopped loving me and lifting me. I adore each of you so much. (This includes my peeps who have moved to other known parts.)

To a Sertin-family across the pond, you have inspired and challenged and changed me. P.S. The distance sucks.

Bethany Bassett, you are the best "book spouse" a girl could ask for. I could say thank you a million times and it wouldn't feel like enough. You pulled me through, darlin'.

Donna Su, your eyes were invaluable.

Don Jacobson and Matt Baugher, you guys rolled the dice and took a chance on a little-known bandersnatch. I am still astounded and so humbled.

Adria and Anne, you both told me that I had an "amazing mind" and that you loved my book, but you also pushed me so far and hard past my boundaries that I thought I would burst from the stretching. In related news: I am so much better at my job because of it. Thank you, infinitely.

Hey Seth and Amber, aka the Southern version of us, I'm pretty sure it's because y'all saw something in me real early on and decided to spread the word that I even have this book written to begin with. Thank you, my good people.

NOTES

INTRODUCTION: WHY *BANDERSNATCH*?

1. Duns Scotus was a medieval Scottish philosopher and a Franciscan. His idea of thisness is summed up well in Gary S. Rosenkrantz and Joshua Hoffman, *Historical Dictionary of Metaphysics* (Lanham, MD: Scarecrow Press, 2011), 103.

CHAPTER 1: NEW WOR[L]D ORDER

1. "The Great Ones" and "They" are how I sometimes reference the Trinity.

CHAPTER 3: [RE]LEARNING TO DANCE

1. Richard Rohr, *Falling Upward: A Spirituality for the Two Halves of Life* (San Francisco: Jossey-Bass, 2011), 159.

2. I've retold this story from Genesis 2–3 using the dialogue from *The Message* translation.

3. Timothy R. Jennings, *The God-Shaped Brain: How Changing Your View of God Transforms Your Life* (Downers Grove, IL: Intervarsity, 2013), 27.

4. Richard Rohr, *Immortal Diamond: The Search for Our True Self* (San Francisco: Jossey-Bass, 2013), 16.

CHAPTER 4: THE GIFT OF NOT

1. Frederick Buechner, *Secrets in the Dark: A Life in Sermons* (New York: HarperCollins, 2006), 153.

CHAPTER 8: YOU ARE AN ALCHEMIST

1. William Shakespeare, *The Tragedy of Romeo and Juliet* (1594), act 2, scene 2, lines 890–91. OpenSource Shakespeare version, http://www.opensourceshakespeare.org/views/plays/playmenu .php?WorkID=romeojuliet.
2. Quoted by Dorothy Day in *All the Way to Heaven: The Selected Letters of Dorothy Day,* ed. Robert Ellsberg (New York: Crown, 2010), vii.

CHAPTER 9: THE ALCHEMIC POTENTIAL OF DIRTY FEET

1. Elaine N. Aron, *The Highly Sensitive Person: How to Thrive When the World Overwhelms You*, reprint ed. (New York: Broadway Books, 1997).

CHAPTER 10: MEETING JESUS AT FROYO WORLD

1. Quoted in Bert Ghezzi, *Mystics and Miracles: True Stories of Lives Touched by God* (Chicago: Loyala, 2002), 29.

CHAPTER 11: WHERE WAS SOMEBODY?

1. Frederick Buechner, *Listening to Your Life: Daily Meditations with Frederick Buechner* (New York: HarperCollins, 1992), April 10.

CHAPTER 14: YOU MADE ME LOOK AT YOU

1. Frederick Buechner, *The Hungering Dark* (San Francisco: HarperSanFrancisco, 1969), 13.
2. Shane Claiborne, Jonathan Wilson-Hartgrove, Enuma Okoro, *Common Prayer: A Liturgy for Ordinary Radicals* (Grand Rapids: Zondervan, 2010), 48.

CHAPTER 15: CRACK HOUSE FAMILY

1. This phrase is a common refrain in book 7 of C. S. Lewis's Chronicles of Narnia series: *The Last Battle* (New York: HarperCollins, 2007).

CHAPTER 16: CROSS-DRESSERS AND KUMBAYAS

1. Fyodor Dostoyevsky, *The Brothers Karamazov,* trans. Constance Garnett (New York: Modern Library, 1996), 356–57.

CHAPTER 17: REDEFINING ART (LIFE AS ART)

1. Frederick Buechner, *Now and Then: A Memoir of Vocation* (San Francisco: HarperSanFrancisco, 1983), 87.
2. Frederick Buechner, *The Alphabet of Grace* (San Francisco: HarperSanFrancisco, 1970), 36.

CHAPTER 18: MARRIAGE AS ART

1. Frederick Buechner, *The Hungering Dark* (San Francisco: HarperSanFrancisco, 1969), 90–91.
2. Madeleine L'Engle, *Walking on Water: Reflections on Faith and Art,* Wheaton Literary Series (Colorado Springs: Waterbrook, 2001), 193–94.

CHAPTER 20: SPIRITUALITY AS ART

1. Kent Nerburn, ed., *The Wisdom of the Native Americans* (Novato, CA: New World Library, 1999), 86.
2. Quoted in Kevin Burke, ed., *Pedro Arrupe: Essential Writings* (Maryknoll, NY: Orbis, 2004), 8. The editor affirms that this quote is attributed to Father Arrupe.
3. Quoted in Tim Young, "Life Is a Beautiful Struggle," *Heartstone Journey* (blog), June 10, 2014, http://heartstonejourney.com /life-is-a-beautiful-struggle/.

CHAPTER 21: DO YOU BELIEVE IT?

1. Mary Oliver, "The Summer Day," *New and Selected Poems*, vol. 1 (Boston: Beacon Press, 1992), 94.

ABOUT THE AUTHOR

Credit: Desirea Still

Erika Morrison is a writer and speaker, a visionary and life artist. With an unconventional and poetic approach to spirituality, she paints bold, prophetic portraits of kingdom-come. Erika makes her home and invests her heart in the Yale University town of New Haven, Connecticut, along with her husband, Austin; their sons, Gabe, Seth, and Jude; and a female pit bull named Zeppelin.